Fifth Edition by Tim Moshansky

Published by First Wave Publishing
Box 172, Lions Bay, BC
VON 2E0

Printed in Canada
ISBN 978-0-9680702-4-6

MIX
Paper from responsible sources
FSC® C016245

The text and cover is printed on chlorine-free paper with vegetable based inks paper meeting the requirements of the Forest Stewardship Council (www.fsc.org).

This book is published without the help of any government subsidies or loans.
All photos by Tim Moshansky (Except where noted.)

I am happy to present to you the 5th edition of this guide.

The start of a new decade seems to be the perfect time to release a new edition. Filmmaking evolves like a moving target, and new technologies and techniques are continually created to help tell a story in inventive and compelling ways.

This guide is intended to be an overall film production reference for those seeking a career in the industry, and want to know the "lingo" of their craft. Filmmaking is the ultimate collaborative art and it is important to have an understanding of the tools and concepts involved so we are all speaking the same language.

Or you may be someone who just enjoys watching the credits roll by and seeing how many diverse skills and talents are required to create a finished film.

Either way, I hope you enjoy the book and carry it with you wherever you go. If you read it from cover to cover I guarantee you'll sound like you know what you're talking about when you find yourself on a film set, rubbing shoulders with the crew.

"Quiet on the set. Stand by for picture. Lock it up. We're rolling! Scene 5, take 1, A and B camera, mark. Speed! And...action!"

Tim Moshansky
Lions Bay 2012

Legend:

A to Z Guide to Film Terms

Acting

Art

Assistant Directing

Camera

Directing

Editing

Grip

Hair

Lighting

Locations

Make-up

Production costs

Props

Sound

Special FX

Stunts

Transport

T.V.

Wardrobe

Writing

A/B Roll Using two video or film sources running at the same time to create editing effects such as dissolves and wipes.

Abby Singer Shot The second last shot of the day. This term supposedly comes from the 1st A.D. of the same name who would always say, "this is the last shot," when it really wasn't. See also *window shot*.

Above-the-line Production costs that involve the principal creative elements, such as the writer, director, producer and lead performers. See also *below the line*.

Academy Award That highly coveted honour that is bestowed upon filmmakers and actors, as voted on every year by members of the *Academy of Motion Picture Arts and Sciences*. Also called an *Oscar*.

Academy Leader Eight-second countdown at the beginning of films standardised by the *Academy of Motion Picture Arts and Sciences*.

Ace One thousand watt (1k) light.

AC Assistant camera. There are usually 3 assistants for each camera crew: 1st AC is also known as the focus puller, 2nd AC is the "clapper/loader" and the 3rd AC does other tasks including putting down camera and actor "marks," getting lenses and other accessories together and doing runs to the truck.

A.C.E. American Cinematic Editors.

A.C.F.C. Association of Canadian Film Craftspeople.

Action Command for the actors or technicians to begin their performance.

Action Prop Any property or device constructed to perform an action or movement or which has any animated function. The giant squid in *20,000 Leagues Under the Sea* is an action prop. Also called an *animated prop*.

A.C.T.R.A. Alliance of Canadian Cinema, Television and Radio Actors.

Actual Music See *source music*.

Actual Sound Sound that is heard by the characters in a film.

Adaptation An artistic work that has been transferred from one medium to another, and that preserves the artistic integrity of that work. These can include a movie made from a book or a stage play made into a movie and so on. Some of the greatest films of all time have been adaptations, including *Gone with the Wind* and *The Godfather*.

A.D. See *assistant director*.

A.D. Box Small room in the honeywagon trailer for use by the assistant directors, particularly the 3rd A.D., when on location to do paperwork, faxes to the office, etc.

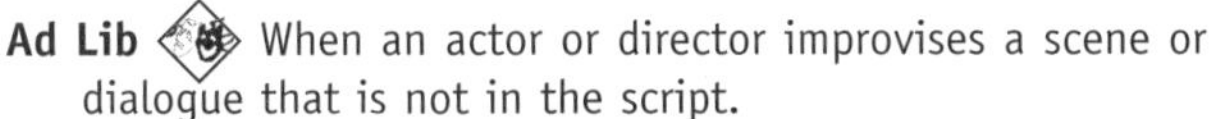

Ad Lib When an actor or director improvises a scene or dialogue that is not in the script.

A.D.R. Automated Dialogue Replacement. The process of re-recording dialogue in a studio to replace or improve the sound quality. See also *looping*.

Aerial Shot A shot that is taken from above the ground with the help of a helicopter, blimp or plane.

AFTRA American Federation of Television and Radio Artists.

Agent A person that represents an actor or performer in exchange for a percentage of the actor's wage or a flat fee. An agent typically negotiates the most money for their client because then they tend to make more.

Air Ram A charged air device that is often used for throwing a stuntman through the air at the same time as an explosion. The air ram is usually placed underneath a platform that an actor or stuntman steps or runs onto, and then is triggered to go off at the appropriate time.

A.K.S. Camera and sound term for a box that contains "all kinds of s**t," or "all kinds of stuff."

Alan Smithee When a director wants his or her name removed from the final credits of a production, usually because of a conflict with the producer or because the show is really awful, the name Alan Smithee is used in place of the director's real name.

Ambient Noise On a sound recording, noise often gets picked up other than the desired dialogue and sound effects, such as traffic, wind, etc. When recording on location, a mixer may record several seconds of ambient noise that reflects the character of the room or space, which is used in the editing process to create a more natural soundscape. Also called *room tone*.

AMPAS Academy of Motion Picture Arts and Sciences. This is the group responsible for giving out the "Oscars" every spring.

Animatronics The area of special effects that deals with puppets of bears, dogs, aliens and humans that are animated with remote controlled servo motors.

Angel Investor Someone who invests money into the making of a film, but who is not involved with the actual film production process and has no creative control.

Answer Print First print of a finished film which is printed with supposedly the correct timing for each shot. Also the first print that has picture and sound combined.

Aperture The size of the hole that lets light into a lens, controlled by the iris.

Apollo A moving camera platform that is like a tulip crane mounted on the back of a truck. The truck can use electric power to move silently during a shot.

Apple Box Small rectangular box used by grips to elevate stands and other work gear. Sizes include full apple, half apple and quarter apple.

Aquarium The control booth or mixing room in a recording studio, named for its large window that looks into the recording room. Also called a *fishbowl*.

Arri Shortened trade name for Arriflex motion picture camera, taken from the first two letters of its inventors, Arnold and Richter.

Art Director Up until the 1970's, the Art Director was the person in charge of preparing and supervising all visual elements on a production. In today's film world, this position has been given the title *Production Designer.* An Art Director now works in most circumstances as an assistant to the PD.

A.S.C. American Society of Cinematographers. A.S.C. is "not a labour union or guild, but an educational, cultural and professional organisation." Membership is by invitation only.

Aside A term that originally comes from the theatre, an *aside* is when a character in a play talks out loud to them-selves and the audience can "listen in" on what they are saying. Other characters in the play do not hear them or notice.

Aspect Ratio The ratio of height to width in a video or film image.

Assembly The physical act of putting together a film or video.

Assistant Director (A.D.) Person(s) who acts as a liaison between the director and the rest of the crew to ensure that everything runs smoothly and on time. See *first assistant director, second assistant director, third assistant director* and *trainee assistant director*.

Assistant Locations Manager (A.L.M.) TO SET Person who oversees a location while shooting. The A.L.M. must possess good P.R. and problem solving skills, and usually has all the relevant information regarding a location such as where to find water, electricity, washrooms and telephones or where to park crew and unit vehicles. The A.L.M. also delegates responsibility to police officers and P.A.'s on set, organises company moves, babysits grumpy crew members and ensures that a location is properly cleaned upon completion of filming. When something goes wrong on a set, the A.L.M. is usually the first person to get dumped on. See also *location manager*.

Associate Producer In the increasingly complex world of filmmaking, sometimes it is hard to understand what each producer actually does. In most cases, an Associate Producer is someone who has been involved in one or more aspects of producing a movie, but is not given full producer credit.

Audition When a performer goes to try out for a role, whether it is for a voice-over or a principal role.

Auteur The "Auteur Theory" was created by French film critics in the 1960's. In a nutshell, it claimed that certain directors merited the title of "auteur," literally the author of the film. Directors such as Hitchcock, Fellini and Truffaut are considered auteurs because of the way their personal style and artistic vision is stamped on every film they created.

Axis Line The imaginary line that is used when filming a scene. The "rule" used in filmmaking is that you should not cross over the Axis because it creates confusion in the viewer when edited together because the actors appear on different sides of the screen. This rule does not apply to a continuous shot that goes *around* the actors. Also called the *180 degree rule*.

B

B-Cam When there is more than one camera on a shoot, they are usually referred to as A-cam, B-cam, and so on, to differentiate between them. A-cam usually takes the most important camera angle for any given shot.

B-Gum A sap from an Olibana tree that is used by special effects personnel to create steam and smoke effects by burning it. See *bee smoker*.

B Movie A low quality, often low budget movie that is characterised by lowbrow subject matter, poor dialogue or script writing and unprofessional actors or crew. These movies often have a limited theatrical release and go straight to video. See also *Cult Classic*.

Babble Crowd background sound that is active and noisy. See also *murmur* and *walla*.

Baby 1) A 1000 watt Fresnel light. 2) A small stand or plate used by grips.

Baby Plate Small plate which can be screwed onto walls and ceilings to mount lights, bounce boards, etc.

Background Extras used in a scene to create a sense of realism.

Backlighting Lighting that comes from behind an actor, towards the camera.

Back Lot TO SET An exterior area on a film studio property where scenes are sometimes filmed, such as crowd scenes or street scenes. A back lot is more controllable and affordable than going out on location, but doesn't always look as convincing as the "real" world.

Ballast A device that regulates the current from a power source to an HMI light.

Bamboolah A rectangular wooden frame with black cloth wrapped around it, used for controlling large unwanted areas of light.

Banana A move performed by the actors or the camera that is in a curved line. "Do a *banana* as you walk by the camera."

Barn Doors The metal doors that you see on the edges of lights, these can be adjusted to control the light from streaming out in all directions.

Barney A padded cover that fits over a camera to prevent camera noise from leaking through. Sometimes a barney may have a heating element to keep the camera warm for cold conditions. Also called a *sound barney*.

Bazooka A long, pole-like device that is used for mounting light fixtures on catwalks.

Beachball See *sandbag*.

Beat A slight pause in speech or action.

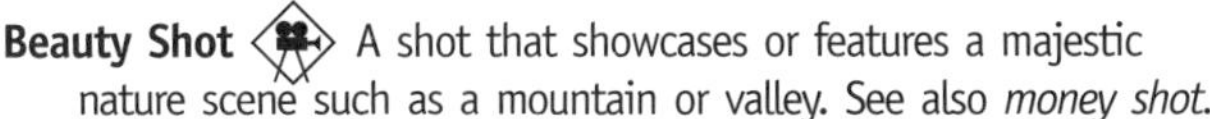

Beauty Shot A shot that showcases or features a majestic nature scene such as a mountain or valley. See also *money shot.*

Bee Smoker A device used for creating small puffs of white smoke, or for creating a hazy, smoke-filled atmosphere on set. These are the same units that bee keepers use to narcotise the bees in an apiary to prevent themselves from being stung.

Below-the-line Production costs that are not included in above the line costs, including crew, equipment, transportation, catering, and so forth.

Best Boy Next in command to a head of department, such as a Best Boy Grip, Lighting or Special Effects.

Betacam A high quality video camera developed and produced by Sony that was used primarily for television productions, ENG and commercials now called *Digital Betacam.*

BFL Technical acronym for Big F#%*ing Light.

Bible The key document used for a television series that contains the character descriptions, story arcs and other key elements of the series for writers, producers and directors to refer to before and during filming.

Big Four The "Big Four" U.S. television networks, as they are often referred to, are ABC, CBS, NBC and Fox.

Bigeye A 10,000 watt (10k) incandescent light.

Biopic A movie whose main plot line concerns itself with a famous person's life story. Movies such as *Chaplin, Amadeus* and *Ray* are considered *biopics.*

Bird's Eye View A camera angle or shot that is high above the set or location so the audience can see everything at once. Hitchcock used this shot in *The Birds* when the gas station explodes into flames. In this case it really is the view from the seagulls looking down.

Bit Part A small speaking part in a movie. Many if not all actors get their start this way. Some make a career out of doing such roles.

Bit Player An actor who makes a brief appearance or has a small speaking role in a film or movie.

Biz Shortened term for the *movie business*.

Black Wrap A thick black aluminum foil used by grips to wrap around barn doors to prevent light from spilling out.

Blimp A hard shell case that fits over the camera to prevent camera noise from escaping. See also *barney*.

Blocking Before filming a new scene, the director arranges a "walk through" of a shot with the actors and key crew members such as the DP, Camera Operators, 1st AD, Gaffer, Key Grip, Set Dresser, Sound Mixer and Boom Operator. Once this "blocking" is complete, the lead actors return to their trailers while the technical crew works out their details for the shot with the stand-ins.

Blonde 2000 watt variable beam spotlight, named for its yellow colour.

Blue Screen An actor is filmed in front of a blue screen so that later a different background may be layered in behind him or her. This technique is also used for miniatures as well. (The "Star Wars" space battle scenes were accomplished using blue screen technology.) See also *composite*.

Body Double A performer that is dressed to look like, or double, an actor in a film. An example would be a shot where we see a character from his or her back entering a building. Often it is a body double that is filmed doing this. Also referred to as a *double* or *photo double*.

Body Mic See *wire*.

Bogie Someone or something (usually a pedestrian or vehicle) that gets in the way of the shot. "Get that *bogie* out of there now!"

Bolex Swiss-made 16mm film camera, known for its ease of operation and dependability.

Bollywood The playful nickname for the huge film industry based in Bombay (now Mumbai), India. Many Indian or "Bollywood" movies feature people dancing and singing in colorful costumes.

Boned Technical term used when something is potentially screwing up and/or delaying some aspect of production. "We're gonna be *boned* if we don't get this shot before sunset."

Boom An extendible pole that holds a microphone to record dialogue and sound effects on a set.

Boom Operator Person who operates the microphone boom, a long, extendible rod with a microphone attached to the end.

Boom Shot A shot where the camera rises or lowers vertically on a platform. See also *crane shot*.

Boot Padded cylindrical sleeve that fits over the viewfinder arm on noisy cameras to prevent sound leakage.

Bosun's Chair A chair attached to a series of pulleys and ropes that can be hung with a camera operator inside to get shots over a river or waterfall, or anywhere a jib arm or dolly track can't go.

Bounce Board A white piece of cardboard or styrofoam used to "bounce" light onto a subject from a direct source, such as the sun or a powered light.

Bounce Light Like a lot of motion picture lighting, this is light that is bounced off of a reflective surface onto a subject.

Box Office The total amount of money raised by the showing of a film in theatres. Also called *box office receipts* or *gross*.

Breakaway Anything that is designed to break apart easily without causing harm to the actors. You often see breakaway chairs and tables in barroom fights in movies.

Breakaway Glass Special glass that is used for stunts and special effects, such as when you see an actor or stuntman crash through a plate glass window. It is essentially special tempered glass that breaks in small pieces rather than dangerous shards. See also *sugar glass*.

Breakdown 1) A term to describe the stressing of props and wardrobe to make them look aged. 2) It also refers to the breakdown of the script into its locations and scenes.

Breaking the Fourth Wall This term comes from theatre and refers to the stage and its three walls, the fourth wall being the invisible barrier at the front of the stage separating between the performers and the audience. To *break the fourth wall* is to address the audience directly, thereby disrupting the artificial world of the play. This also applies to television and movies, when an actor talks directly to the camera, like Bob Hope often did, or as John Cusack's character does in *High Fidelity*.

Break Off/Film Break If a production is shot on film, as opposed to video, there is a certain point each day called the *film break* where the film is sent to the lab to be processed and transferred to be watched as *dailies* or *rushes* the next day.

Break the bubble A term used to describe the tilting of a camera off of the horizontal axis. See also *dutch angle*.

Briefcase Dolly A small, self contained dolly that can be used as a camera or hauling dolly, and packs right up into its own case!

Brute 1) A large flag used for cutting off light. 2) A carbon arc light, broken down into a baby brute and a lite weight brute.

BTS Behind the Scenes. You may sometimes see this abbreviation on a call sheet, which refers to a small camera crew that will be on set to film documentary style footage of the cast and crew in action. It may also include EPK style interviews with the actors and film crew.

Buck A car or other vehicle that has its top removed for doing interior shots.

Buck and a Half Camera term for 150mm lens.

Buddy Film A film that highlights the relationship between two men who are often forced to work together even though they don't like each other at first. They then go on to battle adversity together and become buddies by the end of the picture.

Buffalo Box Camera housing used to protect a camera when being hand held in rough situations, such as on rollerblades. Also called a *crash box*.

Bumper Television term. It is the short visual segment used in a tv show before and after the commercial breaks.

Burned Location Any location (house, restaurant, park or whatever) that will not allow filming due to previous problems with film crews. Sometimes the result of just too much shooting being done there, a location can also be burned by loud and obnoxious crew members, unfulfilled cash promises, moving trucks in or out after curfew or a multitude of other reasons.

Burn-in Titles or subtitles that are laid on top of an existing film or video image. Once done, these titles cannot be removed, hence the name.

Business The physical actions that an actor does while doing a part, such as fidgeting with a pencil or playing with their hair.

Butt Plug Small metal cylindrical peg that is used to mount small lights.

Butterfly Adjustable board of various sizes attached to two stands so it can be angled to reflect or bounce light.

Buyer A person responsible for buying props or set decorations for the art department of a production company.

Buyout The amount of money paid to an actor in addition to his or her rate that "buys out" the residual pay that would normally come with repeated showings of a tv commercial or tv show.

C-Stand From "Century-stand," this is one of the most useful and used pieces of grip/lighting equipment there is. This "workhorse of the movie industry" has three staggered legs which can be folded under each other in a line for easy storage.

C-47 Technical term for a clothespin. The story goes that a crew member submitted a receipt for clothespins, but it was rejected. He then submitted the receipt for "C-47s" and it was accepted, and the term has been used ever since.

Cable Puller A person in the sound department who is in charge of microphone cables (that sometimes need to be *pulled* out of the way on moving shots) and wiring of actors. Also called a *sound assistant* or *assistant sound mixer.*

Cable Truck The truck that carries and distributes the thick electrical cables for the set.

Call Back After a performer goes for an audition, a *call back* is a sign that he or she were interesting enough to be short-listed, and are requested to come for a subsequent audition. Sometimes an actor may be called back several times before securing a role.

Call Sheet Sheet given out at the end of each day outlining the crew call time for each crew member, and also contains location maps and other production requirements for the next day of shooting.

Call Time The time at which the cast and crew must show up for work on the set. Some crew members may have different call times than others. See also *crew call.*

Cameo A brief appearance or performance (usually by a celebrity) in a film or tv program. Alfred Hitchcock can be seen in a cameo appearance in almost every single one of his films.

Camera Jam That horrific moment when the film gets caught up, or "jammed" within the camera. Also called *salad.*

Camera Operator The person who physically operates or controls the camera during filming. They call out that the camera is rolling, turn the camera off and on, and set the framing for what the camera captures during filming.

Camera Set Up When shooting a scene, many camera set ups are sometimes required to cover each angle. Whenever the camera position changes or the lighting and other elements change, this is called a new set up. A crew may work on only one scene in a day, but they might do anywhere from one to fifty camera set ups.

Camera Truck The truck that houses all of the exposed and unexposed film in coolers, as well as various camera accessories. Usually parked as close to the set as possible.

Cans Slang term for headphones worn by boom operators and sound mixers.

Capsule Gun An air-powered gun that is used to shoot actual pellets or other small ammunition at a target to increase the realism of gunfire on film, often combined with *squib* charges.

Captain See *transport captain*.

Capture The process of transferring video footage from a camera or DV tape to a computer system.

Carps Slang for carpenters, those employed in building the sets.

Cast People portraying the characters in a movie or television program.

Casting The process of finding actors to fill the various roles in a film, usually headed by a casting director.

Casting Couch A reference to the piece of furniture that an aspiring actress or actor has sex on with a director or casting agent in order to secure a role in a film.

Cattle Call A general call for actors or extras.

Catwalk Platforms or decks that are mounted up near the ceiling in many studios. See also *greens*.

Cel A single sheet of celluloid that is used in animation.

Centipede A type of dolly that has a number of small wheels set at an angle to each other that move on a tubular track.

Charlie Bar A long, slender flag used by grips to shade light off a specific area.

Cheat To purposely move an object or actor in or out of the way in coverage shots that may not be exact in continuity, but done in a way so no-one will notice in the final edited version of a film. (e.g. "*Cheat* that table this way a bit so we can see his body more.")

Cheater Plate A small metal plate with an angled rod welded to it. Used for mounting a light so it is at an angle.

Check the Gate The 1st A.D. asks for the camera assistant to "check the gate" when the director has gotten the shot he needs and is ready to move on to the next shot, or wrap for the day. This is done to ensure that the camera gate is clear of small hairs, film shards and other debris.

Cheese Plate A grip term for a metal plate with holes in it that can be used to mount lights, etc. onto almost any surface.

Chick Flick A romantic or heartbreaking movie that appeals specifically to female sensibilities.

Chicken Coop An overhead, box-like multiple light set, usually used for top lighting of sets.

Chimera A small, portable light in a nylon housing. This "soft" light is often used to follow an actor during a moving shot.

Chroma keying To shoot a person or thing with a coloured background so other elements may be layered in where the colour is. For film, a blue screen or green screen is used. Models of spacecraft are often shot against a red screen.

Cinema Verité A genre of cinema that attempts to be as realistic as possible. See also *Neorealism*.

Cinematographer The person responsible for getting the lighting and photographic elements prepared and shot onto film or video. Also called a *director of photography* (DP or DOP).

Circus TO SET The area where the majority of trucks, trailers, tents and catering trucks are set up while filming on location.

Clapper Small black and white board with spaces for the title of the production, the scene number, the take number, the director and cameraman's name, and the name of the production company producing the film. The top of the board has a stick that is clapped together to create a sound and picture reference mark used to synchronise the two later in post production. See also *slate*.

Claw A device within the camera that pulls the film through by the perforations on the side of the film.

Claymation A form of animation that uses clay figures shot one frame at a time to create the illusion of movement when played in real time.

Clean Shot When two actors are facing each other during dialogue scenes, the camera will have a clean angle on each from the angle of the facing actor. A shot is "clean" when the actor facing camera is alone in the frame, and the other actor is off camera. A shot is "dirty" when it contains part of the actor with his back to the camera, also called an "over the shoulder" shot.

Closed Set For filming a scene that requires actor nudity or an intense emotional commitment, the director will call for a *closed set,* in which only the absolutely essential crew members (such as the camera and boom operator) may be present.

Clunker Box A device used for sequentially firing lights, squibs or explosions. The predecessor of the clunker box is the nail board, which some special effects people still prefer.

Cobweb Juice Liquid, glue-like solution used by special effects people to create cobwebs.

Cobweb Spinner A drill-like device with fan blades attached to it that is used for creating cobwebs.

Coffin Light A set of lights arranged with a black curtain around them for soft lighting of a scene.

Coke and a Smoke When the director wants a private blocking or rehearsal with the actors, the crew is asked to go for a "coke and a smoke," i.e. leave the set and take a break.

Cold Reading Reading a script or line without seeing it or previously rehearsing it.

Colour Bars A standard set of colours arranged in bars on a tv screen used to achieve an accurate colour setting. You sometimes see these on tv when you wake up on the couch at 4 a.m.

Colourist The person in the post production department that digitally "tweaks" or adjusts the colour and contrast of specific shots or sequences within a film. See also *digital intermediate*.

Colour Temperature A method of determining the colour of a light by its temperature. This temperature is measured in the Kelvin scale, which is the same as the metric Celsius scale, but with a different starting point. (0°K=-273°Centigrade).

Colour Timer The person who works with the final film print to ensure the right balance and intensity of colour for each shot or scene within a movie.

Comedy A genre of film that is intended to make an audience laugh.

Commentative Sound Sound heard only by the audience, not by the characters in a film. This includes background music and narration.

Common Marker When two or more cameras use the same clapper board to mark the beginning or end of a shot.

Company Move TO SET When shooting on location, sometimes it is necessary to move the entire crew and all of the trucks to a new location. This may sound easy but more closely approximates organised confusion. Not to be confused with a mini move.

Completion Guarantee $ A guarantee or bond from a bank or financier that ensures there are funds in place to be able to finish a project with an approved cast, script and budget, and that a producer will deliver a finished product to the distributor. Also called a *completion bond*.

Completion Guarantor The person or company that has a bond in place to ensure a movie has enough money to be completed.

Composite Two or more images that have been layered together to form a single image. This technique is often used for special effects.

Com-Tek Small device used to receive an audio signal so the director and other key personnel can monitor the dialogue and sound as they are being recorded.

Condor Large, movable crane-like device with a bucket on an extending arm to elevate cameras, lights and/or operators. Not to be confused with the Robert Redford movie *Three Days of the Condor*.

Continuity The flow of narrative within a film. If continuity is not right, audiences are left wondering what happened from one edit to the next.

Contrapuntal Music Background music that is not synchronised to the image on the screen, but runs its own course, as if it were telling its own version of the story. See *Mickey Mousing*.

Cookie Cutter See *cuculoris*.

Co-Producer Someone who shares the producer credit for a movie or tv program with someone else.

Co-Production A production that is jointly produced by two entities, whether they are corporations, countries or individuals. Also called a *co-pro*.

Copy Walkie-talkie talk for: "I understood your message," or, "Got it." "Do you *copy* that?"

Costume Designer Person who, in consultation with the director and production designer, designs, creates or acquires all wardrobe and costumes needed for a production. They also ensure that extra sets of clothing in the right sizes are available for stunt and photo doubles and stand-ins.

Costumer You will often find this person in the wardrobe trailer organising and issuing costumes to actors and extras. Other duties include washing, drying and ironing of costumes.

Costume Supervisor Person who is in charge of all wardrobe requirements on a set. They check wardrobe continuity before shooting, do "final touches," and keep the actors warm and dry between takes. They also assist in the final decision as to what the extras will wear while on set.

Coverage During a shoot, getting "coverage" refers to the amount of angles and viewpoints captured on film that can be used in the editing process to give a scene pace, variety and movement.

Cover Set TO SET A pre-dressed studio or location set that sits waiting and is used to "cover" for a production in case of bad weather or logistical problems. Also called *weather cover.*

Cowboy Shot A medium wide shot of an actor from above their cowboy hat to about halfway between his waist and knees. This term comes from the western movies, where a shot would frame the cowboy from the top of his head to just below his gun and holster.

Crab Dolly Four-wheeled camera dolly that can move in any direction (including sideways, like a crab).

Craft Service 1) The area (usually a table) where all kinds of food and drink are served on a continual basis all day long for everyone in the cast and crew. You can generally find crew members who aren't currently busy grazing in this area. 2) The person on the set who has industrial first aid training for any accidents or injuries that may occur, and who prepares and serves foods and snacks to the crew throughout the working day. Also may be shown on the call sheet as FACS, CSFA, or Craft Service/First Aid.

Crane Shot A shot which is achieved by raising the camera and operator(s) with a crane or similar device. It is often used as the first or last shot of a feature film.

Crew Call That point in time when the majority of the crew is on the set and working "on the clock."

Crystal Sync True, reliable 24 frames per second camera speed.

CTB Colour Temperature Blue. A lighting term that refers to the blue gel used in front of lights. CTB is used for correcting tungsten light for daylight film. A CTB comes in a full, half, quarter and eighth intensity.

CTO Colour Temperature Orange. A lighting term that refers to the orange gel used in front of lights. A full, half, quarter or eighth CTO gel is used to correct or alter the light from the sun for tungsten-rated film.

C.U. Close-up. A shot that frames an actor's face.

C.S.C. Canadian Society of Cinematographers.

Cuculoris Patterned flag that is used to create shadow patterns on backgrounds and subjects. Lighting directors frequently use them to simulate sunlight filtering through trees. Also called a *cookie cutter*, or *cukaloris*.

Cue A signal for an actor, stuntman or extra to begin movement or speech.

Cue Card Large board with writing on it, usually lines or prompts for the actors.

Cue Sheet During the editing process, a cue sheet is used to keep track of the sequence of edits, the times, various tracks of sound and dialogue and so forth.

Cult Classic, Cult Movie A movie that develops a "cult" following of fans and viewers. Most cult classics (often lower-budget films) have some kind of quirkiness or novelty about them that makes them endearing. One of the most obvious examples is the hugely popular and successful *Rocky Horror Picture Show,* which still plays at midnight in repertory movie houses all over the world.

Cut 1) What the director yells when he wants the cameras and sound to stop rolling. 2) An edit in a film or video.

Cutaway A shot or edit that literally cuts away from the primary action, used to relieve tension or boredom during a scene.

Cutter 1) An editor, or one who cuts and and then splices the film together. 2) A grip term for a device that is used to cut off light from a subject.

Cutting room floor Where you and your ego end up if an editor cuts you out of a film.

Cyclorama (Cyc) A large, curved backdrop used to represent sky in a studio.

Cyc-strip A long strip of lights used for even illumination of a cyclorama.

A **Towable Genny**, or Generator provides all of the power for a film shoot while on location. These are extremely sophisticated pieces of machinery that need to run at exactly 60 Hz so power is constant for lights and other film gear. Sometimes several **gennies** may be used for larger shoots or night lighting. © 2010

Dailies Unedited, raw footage, usually shown in a small screening room to the producers, directors, and other key personnel to see if what they filmed the previous day is acceptable.

Dance Floor Smooth, pristine sheets of plywood that are screwed onto less expensive plywood for the camera dolly to move on.

Dash Card Card used to identify crew members' cars while filming on location.

D.A.W. Digital Audio Workstation. A state of the art editing system that can edit digital sound and pictures into finished, complete productions using just a computer.

Day-and-Date A movie that is simultaneously released in movie theatres, as a DVD, and as video-on-demand.

Day for Night Shooting a scene during the day which actually appears in the movie as a night scene. This may be done in a variety of ways, including using different film stock, filters or developing procedures, or if shooting indoors, by blanketing out all windows and doors and lighting accordingly. Often appears as D/N on call sheets.

Day out of Days (D.O.O.D.) A document prepared by the A.D. department that lists each day in a production and a brief description of scenes, including actors and locations required.

Day Player A day player is an actor hired on a daily basis. This actor only has a few lines or scenes. The day player must be notified that they are finished by the end of the day; otherwise they are automatically called back for another day of work.

Day Mo Crew member working on the set on a temporary, daily basis. A slightly condescending term.

Dead Cat The name for an artificial-fur "sock" that fits over a microphone to reduce wind noise when recording sound. See also *windjammer* and *zeppelin windscreen*.

Dead Kitten A smaller version of the dead cat. See above.

Deal Memo The contract you sign with a production company prior to beginning work that outlines how much you will be paid, what screen credit you will receive and other details.

Deep Focus A process developed in the 1940's with faster film and more powerful lighting, making it possible to keep a greater depth of a scene in focus, even in interiors.

Deferral A contract method (often used by low budget producers) used to defer wages to cast and crew and equipment payments until a film has been released and makes a profit.

Depth of Field The amount of focus of near and distant objects in a camera lens.

Descender A device developed by British paratroopers to control the rate of descent of an actor on a cable, which is used by special effects people.

Desert Dolly Sometimes called by its trade name, the Mojave Desert Dolly has big balloon tires that can travel over sandy beaches, deserts and other loose earth. Primarily used for lighting and grip equipment more than as a camera dolly.

Desmond A T-stop of 2.2, i.e. *two two*, named for the South African Nobel Prize winner Desmond Tutu. This term originated in South Africa but has since travelled to North America and is widely used today.

Development The very early stage of a production when the script is being prepared by the writer(s) and directors and actors are being suggested for the project. Often a film or television studio will give money to a writer or director, to develop the story material and presentation. This is called a *development deal*

D.G.A. Director's Guild of America.

D.G.C. Director's Guild of Canada.

Dialogue (Dialog) The words spoken by the characters in a film.

Dialogue Coach The person who coaches or helps actors who need to speak with an accent or foreign dialect in a film.

Dialogue Editor The post-production sound person whose job it is to find the best lines of dialog from the best individual takes and smoothly blend them into the final soundtrack.

Diffusion A reduction in the intensity of a light, or the device that does this (e.g. opal, litegrid, 216, frost).

DI See below.

Digital Intermediate (DI) The process of digitizing the final edited version of a film or video production. A *DI*, as it is often called, allows for final colour, contrast and other image adjustments via digital software tools, and is the last stage before duplication and distribution of a project to theatres and other consumer formats.

Dimmer A device used to vary the intensity of lights. See also *variac*.

Dingle An item, usually a tree branch, that is dangled in front of a light to create shadows on a subject.

Dinosaur Board The name given to the old style "boards" used by the assistant directors to arrange the shooting schedule. The actors, sets and other requirements are written on little strips that fit into the board.

Direct Cut A cut that is used for geographical or temporal (time) leaps in a film. It is also called an *impact cut*.

Director The head honcho. The big cheese. The auteur. The director, as we all know, is the person ultimately responsible for the look, sound and emotional impact of a film. He or she is the person who assembles a cast and crew often totaling over a hundred people to assist them in creating their vision of the film. A director directs the action of the actors, consults with the wardrobe, effects, lighting, grip, art, sound and locations department heads and with the help of the director of photography places the camera(s) in various positions to shoot scenes that will eventually be edited into a complete motion picture.

Director's Cut The final edit of a film by a director that most closely resembles their vision for the movie. The reason the *director's cut* has become so popular in recent years is because audiences found out that producers and studio heads often had the final word on how a film would be edited and released. They were trimming scenes just to shorten the length without any regard to how that affects the flow of the film.

Dissolve Two shots that overlap each other in a final print are called a *dissolve*. The term can also be used as a verb, as in, "the shot of the car *dissolves* into the close-up of her face."

Distribution Once a film or tv show has been completed, it becomes necessary to distribute the product to networks and theatres for broadcast. In most cases, a show will already have a distribution deal in place before it starts production.

Ditty Bag Small bag used by film crews to store little tools and other items. This term arose from sailors who carried a ditty bag of necessary items while at sea.

Diving Board Small wooden platform that attaches to the front or side of a dolly for a camera operator to stand on, hence the term. It also extends ahead of the dolly and is not used as commonly as the regular "side board".

Docudrama A documentary show that uses professional actors, props, sets and production value to explain or present a story, often within a traditional documentary framework. This technique often works quite well for historical documentaries.

Documentary (Doc) A type of program or film that uses non-fictional subject matter and (usually) non-professional actors to inform, teach or sway the audience. Docs often use a narrator to help guide the story.

Dolly Platform on wheels that has a mount for a camera, and can be pushed or pulled to create a smooth movement. Dollies are often put on tracks, and the camera and operator(s) ride with it. A crab dolly is a complex unit that can do tricky steering maneuvers and can rise up and down via hydraulics.

Dolly Grip Grip crew member specialising in camera movements via dollies of various kinds.

Dolly Track A tubular track that is used to guide a camera dolly for smooth "tracking" shots.

Donut Small, round pad with a hole in it that fits over the eyepiece of a viewfinder, or the larger round pad that fits between the matte box and lens of a camera to prevent light from getting in.

D.O.P. Director of Photography. A D.O.P. works closely with the lighting and camera departments to create the images that will eventually appear onscreen. Also called a *DP*.

Doorway Dolly A small, wagon like dolly that is steered by a pull handle. Used for cameras and operators.

Dope Sheet A list of the exposed contents of a film canister or videotape, or a list of shots or scenes from a movie that have already been completed.

Dot A small round "flag" used by grips to block out a small section of light.

Double 1) A member of the cast who "doubles," or impersonates the real actor. See also photo double and stunt double. 2) Grip term for a net diffusion, with 2 pieces overlapped. 3) Lamp Op term for a wire scrim.

Double Dip To work on two shows (and therefore collect two paycheques) at the same time.

Drama A film that tells a story in a straightforward way. The emphasis in a drama is on characters, family, emotions and the life experience.

Drawdown Large sums of money are often needed to produce a film. As various stages of a film are reached, they trigger funds that are released by the bank or financier to be used for that portion of the process. For example, opening a production office and beginning "prep" might be one activator, and the first day of principal photography would be another, and so on. These are called *drawdowns*.

Dress To decorate and arrange items such as furniture, drapes and artwork on a set.

Drive-by A shot where a camera shoots a stationary subject from a moving vehicle.

Dry run A rehearsal of a scene without shooting any film.

Dubbing 1) Replacing sound with a more complete, or better soundtrack mix. 2) The replacement of foreign dialogue in film with English, or vice-versa.

Dub Stage The sound studio where the dialog, music and effects tracks are mixed together.

Duece A two-thousand watt (2k) light.

Dulling Spray A spray used on shiny surfaces such as windows and mirrors to prevent unwanted reflections.

Duster Slang term for a western/cowboy film.

Dust Gun A gun used by special effects people to create clouds of dust on a set.

Dutch Angle An exaggerated camera angle tilted to the right or left of the horizontal line, popularised by early Dutch film-makers. Also called an *oblique angle*.

Dutch Head Tripod head that can pan, tilt and rock at angles other than 90 degrees. Also called a *rock and roll head*, this unit is very popular for rock videos.

Duvetyne Trade name for fire retardant black cloth that is used by grips on flags and windows to block out light.

D.V.E. Digital video effects.

E.C.U. Extreme close-up.

Edge of Frame The extent to which the camera lens sees in every direction.

Editing The assembling of images and sound into a completed production. One of the least understood aspects of production, editing is an extremely important and powerful part of the filmmaking process. It is here that the show is shaped and molded into its final form.

Editor A person who is involved in any part of the assembling of raw images and sound into a final product. There are a myriad of different types of editors, including dialog, special effects and music editors for sound and dozens of people involved with picture editing.

E.F.P. Electronic field production. E.F.P. is known for having somewhat better production values than E.N.G.

1/8th Pages in a script are broken down into eighths (1/8's) of a page. A certain scene might run for 4 and 2/8, which means four and two eighths of a page. This makes it easier to schedule a movie or TV production for shooting.

Eighty Six (86) To take something away. E.g. "We'll have to *86* the catering truck before the next setup." This term comes from bylaw 86 in Los Angeles which stipulates that film crews have to be out of residential neighbourhoods by a certain time.

Electrics See *lighting department*.

Electronic Press Kit (E.P.K.) A press kit that is in the form of a video. A small crew, usually consisting of an interviewer, cameraman and sound person, shoots promotional footage and "behind the scenes" segments on movie sets for television shows (like "E.T.") or "the making of" programs. 2) This term is also being used for websites that offer a downloadable EPK for music artists and films.

Elevator Shot A shot that involves moving the camera on a platform vertically up or down, but not horizontally.

Emmy The *Emmy Awards* are given out each year to the best and brightest involved in television production and broadcasting. There are many categories recognized by the Emmy's, including the *Daytime Emmy's, Primetime Emmy's, Sports Emmy's* and so on.

Ensemble Cast A movie or television show that has several "stars" in the cast, where each character is given nearly equal screen time and dialogue. Films such as The *Magnificent Seven, Kelly's Heroes* and *Pulp Fiction* have an *ensemble cast*.

E.N.G. Electronic News Gathering. A style of filming that is used by small news crews on location, usually consisting of just a camera operator and sound person.

E & O Errors and Omissions. A clause in a legal insurance contract for a film company that allows for errors that occur that were unforeseen, such as a logo that is accidentally filmed in a shot.

Episodic A series of half or one-hour programs that are shown each week on television for a specific duration of weeks (called a *season*) or released as a "set" of programs.

Establishing Shot A wide shot of a location or set that gives the audience a reference point to where the scene is taking place. This type of shot is often shown at the beginning of a scene, like a full shot of a building. Not to be confused with a *master shot*.

Executive Producer 1) The credit given to someone who either contributes or raises the majority of finances for a production or 2), is responsible for creative input such as writing the screenplay or creating a series.

EXT. Exterior. A shot that takes place outdoors.

Extra A person who is cast in a production, but who has no spoken lines. Extras are sometimes referred to as *B.G*, or *background performers*.

Extras Holding The place where extras are held until they are required for a scene.

Eyelight A small light which is used to create highlights in an actor's eyes.

Eyeline Where an actor is looking during a take. It is important to keep his or her eyeline clear during filming to avoid possible disruption of concentration.

Eyemo Small 35mm camera body that is used primarily for running at very high speeds for slow-motion photography. They are great for burying in the ground to shoot a herd of cattle running by.

F-stop Represents the light transmitting capabilities of a lens, a number of measurement obtained by dividing the focal length of a lens by its aperture.

Fade-In/Out A transition, or fade from a black or white background into a video or film image or vice-versa.

Favoured Nations When everybody from a creative team is paid equally. For instance the actors in a movie or the writers of a tv series. During the filming of the comedy tv show *SCTV*, there was an agreement to have Favoured Nations in place for the stars, but it was later revealed that some people were being paid more than others.

F.D.R. Another term for new deal, to signify that a shot has been completed and the crew is moving on to something else. This term arose from the fact that Franklin D. Roosevelt supposedly would always call for a new deal while he was president.

Feature A movie length film that is shown in movie houses or released on video. A feature can be shot on 16 or 35mm film, DV or digital film and is usually at least 90 minutes long.

Fernie Another term for furniture pad, an all purpose pad used by grips to protect furniture, camera equipment or actors, and by the sound dept. to deaden unwanted noise.

Fill Light An extra light used to add, or fill areas of a set not lit by a key light.

Filmanthropy While at the 2007 Sundance Film Festival, Ted Leonsis coined the phrase *filmanthropy* to describe investing in films that analyse and illuminate important issues around the world and benefit a social cause.

Filmic Time The measurement of time as it occurs to the characters in a film. This may only take a fraction of actual time to watch.

Film Noir A style of film that deals with a bleak, dark subject matter and is often filmed in black and white with plenty of shadows. This style was developed and rose to popularity in the 1940's and 1950's, with films such as *Casablanca*, *Rebecca* and *Spellbound*.

Filmography A list of movies by a certain director or producer, or of actors or crew who worked on the films. A *filmography* usually starts with the first film appearance or debut and lists any other movies right up until the present day.

Final Cut The final, finished edit of a movie or film that will be seen by audiences. See also *rough cut*.

Final Cut Pro Software that is used to digitally edit sound and picture for movies and tv shows.

Final Touches The 1st A.D. calls for final touches just before the camera will roll, giving the set dec, wardrobe, hair, make-up and prop departments a last chance to tweak their subjects and make last minute adjustments.

Finger A long, thin flag used by grips to block a small portion of light on a subject.

Fire in the Hole When an explosion, fire or gunfire is used on set, this phrase is called out to let the crew know it loaded and ready to go. See also *hot*.

Fire Watch When a crew breaks for lunch, a P.A. is assigned to watch the set and all of the equipment to ensure nothing is stolen or damaged. This term harks back to the old studio days when there was an actual danger of fire starting out and burning everything down.

First Assistant Director (1st A.D.) The person responsible for ensuring that all of the departments are organised, co-ordinated and logistically ready for shooting scenes on a movie set. In pre-production they prepare a script breakdown and shooting schedule in consultation with the department heads. On set they assist the director by arranging all of the details so they can concentrate on the actors and the scene itself. They can often be identified by the headsets they wear to communicate with the crew, or as the person who calls out, "roll sound," "roll cameras," "cut," "reset," or "that's a wrap folks."

First Positions Return to your original positions after a cut. This term applies to actors, animals, extras and vehicles.

First Team The main actors. The 1st A.D. calls for the *first team* when everything is set and ready to roll.

Fishbowl See *aquarium*.

Fishpole Slang name for a boom, or microphone pole.

F.I.Z. Camera term for focus, iris, zoom.

Flag Square Black flag in a metal frame used to totally block out sections of light.

Flame Bar Long bar with handle that is used by special effects crews to simulate fire and flames in a controlled manner.

Flaming Sidewinder Slang for a stunt/special effect in which a car is filmed driving up to another car or object, hitting a ramp that launches the car into the air and into a side spin where it blows up in a ball of flames.

Flare An unwanted bright reflection that shows up on film.

Flashback A segment of a film which refers back to an earlier part of the narrative.

Flat A lightweight, movable 4′ x 8′ wooden structure that is used as part of a wall or backdrop in a studio or set.

Flatbed Another term for a Steenbeck editing table.

Flick Slang for *movie*. This term arose from the fact that a projector "flickers" with light as the film is run through it.

Flub To accidentally miss or screw up a line of dialogue.

Fluid Head A tripod head that uses a fluid to aid in smooth camera movements.

Fly To hang lights or rigging from the ceiling of a studio.

Flying in Phrase used by crew members to let someone know that they are on their way in to a set immediately.

Flying Moon A large lighting unit that houses four 25k HMIs and is raised above a set 100 feet or so to simulate artificial moonlight.

Focal Length The distance from the optical centre of the lens to the filmplane when the lens is focused at infinity.

Focus Puller Camera assistant who adjusts the focus of the lens while filming, often needed because the camera operator simply can't do everything at once. Also known as *1st camera assistant*.

Fog Filter A filter placed over the camera lens to simulate fog on film.

Foley Named after its creator, Jack Foley, this is the art of creating sound effects in a recording studio, whether walking on various surfaces to create footstep sounds, or clanging glasses in a bar scene in time to the action on the screen.

Foley Artist Person who creates Foley sounds for a film.

Foley Stage A room in a recording studio used for recording Foley sounds. It usually has a series of square panels on the floor which, when removed, reveal different textured surfaces such as concrete, sand, gravel and hard wood for a foley artist to match footstep sounds.

Follow-shot Any shot which follows an actor or vehicle, whether with panning, dollying, or any combination of movement.

Footage The amount of film used during a shoot is measured by the foot. The term is now used to describe any moving image captured by a camera, even if no actual "film" is even used. You might hear someone say, "We got some great *footage* of that car chase today."

Foot Candle Measurement of the intensity of a light source.

Force Majeur An unexpected or uncontrollable situation that causes a show to shut down filming for a period of time. This could be an actor getting ill, a freak weather occurrence such as a snowstorm, or other similar reason.

Forced Call When a production manager needs to bring in a cast and crew without giving them a specific amount of time between wrap and their call time the next morning or over a weekend. To compensate for this, the crew and cast being "forced" are paid a premium rate for the entire day.

Foreground Anything that is in the front of a camera's field of vision and not blocked by anything else.

Fourth Wall The theatre gives us this phrase which means the imaginary "wall" at the front of a stage which looks out to the audience. Normally actors in a play only talk to each other. To "break the fourth wall" means to talk directly to the audience.

fps Frames per second.

Frame Grab A still image that has been taken from a single frozen or paused video or film image.

Frame 1) The perimeter of vision recorded by a camera. 2) What the camera operator calls out once they have set the framing for the shot they want and are ready for the actors to begin.

Freeze Frame An image that has been stopped during a moving picture, allowing viewers to view a "frozen" image. The *freeze frame* is often used behind the titles or credits of a film or tv show.

French Flag A small, opaque shade for shielding the camera lens.

French Hours A shooting day that allows for a one-hour sit down breakfast followed by nine hours of shooting without a break, at which point wrap is called. Food is served to the crew at various points during the day, and they grab a quick bite as they are working. This arrangement was developed and popularised in Europe, but is also used in North America to get a production back on schedule after an extremely long day, or for lighting reasons. Also called *Pacific Northwest Hours*.

French New Wave A group of artistic and innovative French filmmakers from the late 1950's and early 1960's which included Jean-Luc Godard, Claude Chabrol, Francois Truffaut and others. Movies from this group feature (at the time) radical cinema techniques such as long takes, jump cuts, improvised dialogue, breaking the axis, hand held shots and talking directly to the camera. They were also characterised by philosophical themes such as existentialism and the importance of the individual.

French Reverse A reverse shot that cheats the angle because of some unwanted background.

Fresnel 1) A type of convex lens used for focusing lights. 2) A light equipped with a Fresnel lens. (pronounced fre-nell.)

Frost An opaque sheet of plastic in a frame used to diffuse a light source.

Fuller's Earth A non-toxic, clay-based earth used on movie sets as a double for real dirt.

Futz To alter or add sound to a dialogue track to make it sound like the voice is coming over the radio or a telephone.

F/X See *special effects.*

The **Cable Truck** transports and distributes electrical cables that power the set.

Behind the Scenes

Street scenes are often shot on a film studio **backlot.** Shooting scenes here gives filmmakers more control and flexibility as opposed to filming on a real location. Right behind the "storefront" facades is a soundstage where sets are built. © 2010

A **boom operator** records the clapper at the beginning of a take. This helps editors synchronize the sound and picture during the editing process. ©2010

A well-worn **apple box** – one of the most common and useful pieces of film gear there is. © 2010

Various lighting **diffusion gels** all lined up and ready to go. © 2010

The **donut** is the name given to the soft, leathery cushion that fits over the viewfinder to make it more comfortable for the camera operator. © 2010

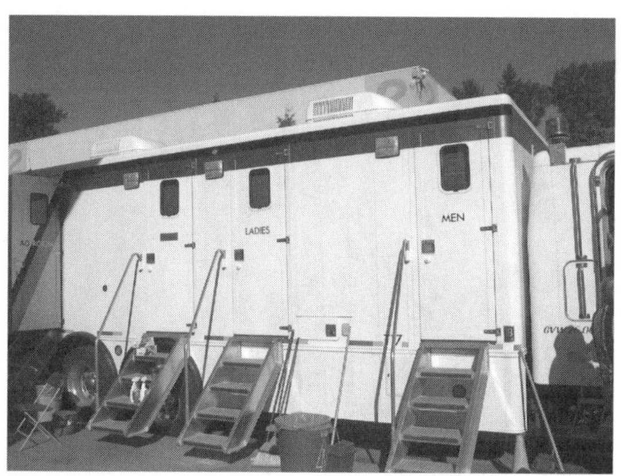

The all-important **honeywagon** for when you need to go 10-100 on location. © 2010

Apple boxes of various sizes, including full, half and quarter apples. © 2010

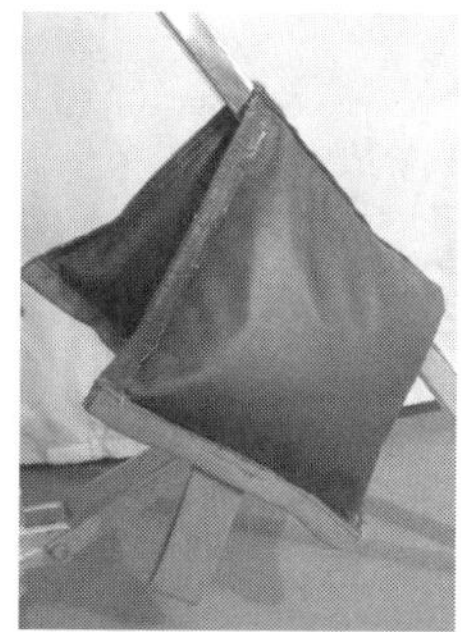

A **beachball**, or **sandbag** is used to stabilise a light stand. © 2010

A huge **HMI** 12k light is used to recreate sunlight on a busy city street location. © 2010

A **Genie Lift** gets a light high up to shine through the windows of a location. Photo by: Joseph MacKinnon © 2010. Used with permission.

Car mounts are used to film actors as they drive. In this case a side-mount or **hostess tray** is used to film through the passenger window. Photo courtesy of Matthews Studio Equipment. © 2010. Used with permission.

Dolly grips and **focus pullers** assist on a two-camera setup. © 2010

A crew finishes a **crane shot** of a car driving down a street. Crane shots are often used at the beginning or end of a movie or scene. Check out the great crane shots at the beginning of Orson Welles' *A Touch of Evil* or the ending of Roman Polanski's *Chinatown*.
Photo by: Karl Herrmann © 2010. Used with permission.

Stills Photographer on set
Photo by: Joseph MacKinnon © 2010. Used with permission.

A production **Sound Mixer** listens to the dialog as it is being recorded on set. © 2010

Lights illuminating a set. Notice the **translight** on the right hand side, or large translucent photograph, which is used in this case to simulate a water view without having to go on location. © 2010

A **Steadicam** camera operator checks his framing during a shot. The Steadicam is also known as a camera stabilising device. © 2010

A close-up shot of a **centipede dolly** that allows for smooth, stable tracking shots.
Photo courtesy of
Matthews Studio Equipment.
© 2010. Used with permission.

A **C-Stand** with a **knuckle** on top for holding flags, diffusion and cutters. © 2010

Gaffer The person in charge of all electrical and lighting requirements on set. This name comes from the early days of theatre in Britain, when all of the lighting was provided by candles. The lighting person would use a long stick called a gaff to light all of the candles, and was therefore called a "gaffer." His son, whom he would teach the trade, was called the "best boy."

Gag A joke, effect or contraption that is employed during a shot.

Gag Reel An edited portion of out-takes from a production, usually shown to the crew at wrap parties or at the end of a shooting schedule.

Gak General film term for equipment, props, etc. "Keep an eye on that gak so no-one touches it."

Gak Truck See *slush truck*.

Gaffer Tape Strong tape used by almost every department on a set. Sometimes called *duct tape,* this product was popularised by the character on the tv series *MacGyver,* who used it to get out of any situation. To

"MacGyver" something has become part of our common speech.

Gap Financing To finance a production through a combination of various sources, including bank loans, venture capital, and tax credits.

Garbage Matte A term used by editors and visual effects people for a shot done live that will be turned into a composite shot with computer elements added in later. They call it a garbage matte because it is not a clean or true matte, but one that calls for a great deal of manipulation to create the final shot.

Gate Check See *check the gate.*

Gels Coloured gelatin sheets that are placed in front of lights to change colour or colour intensity.

Genny Generator. A very important piece of film equipment– without it not much could be done on a modern film set (i.e. power for lights, fans, hair dryers, etc.).

Genny Operator Person in charge of running and maintaining the generator.

Genre A specific type or style of movie. Some typical genres include horror, action, drama, comedy and other types of films. Also called *cinematic genre,* there are three subcategories that movies may fit into, including those of setting (i.e. science fiction or westerns), mood (i.e. suspense or horror) or format (i.e. musical or action).

Gimbal Platform used to simulate movement in any type of vehicle, whether it is a car, plane, boat or spaceship.

Gimmick Light A small bulb used for hiding in confined spaces. Also called a *peanut bulb*.

Giraffe Boom A flexible microphone boom on a tripod used in studio situations as opposed to a fishpole.

Glidecam Similar to a *Steadicam*, a *Glidecam* is a camera stabilising device that is worn by the camera operator to achieve smooth movement or tracking shots.

Glow Light A very weak light source used to make an actor's face glow.

Gobo 1) Any shield or device that keeps light from directly striking the camera lens. 2) A free-standing structure used to disperse sound in any given environment.

Gobo Arm A thin, cylindrical extension arm to raise flags, etc. Usually mounted on a C-stand with a knuckle.

Gobo Ball A small rubbery ball that fits on the end of a gobo arm to prevent injuries to the cast and crew.

Go-Motion Computer controlled rods attached to a puppet allows it to be controlled and filmed in real time. See also *stop motion*.

Go to "2" When communicating with walkie talkies, channel "1" is reserved for the entire crew to give short requests and commands to each other. When a longer conversation is required or when the topic does not concern everybody, you may hear someone say, "go to 2," which means change your radio to channel two.

Greek To change a sign so it reads differently or cannot be read at all. "If we can't get permission to use their sign we'll *greek* it before we go."

Green Light When a project has been given the go ahead and has the necessary funding in place to begin production. "We've received the *green light* on the feature we've been working on, and we begin production next month."

Green Room Traditionally the room where the talent waits before a performance or television appearance.

Green Screen Coloured screen used on set as a backdrop so CG effects may be added later. See also *blue screen*.

Greens 1) The department responsible for foliage, shrubs and other handling of "green" material that will be a part of a shot. 2) Another word for the catwalks or decks high in the rafters of Hollywood studios, so named because they were painted green.

Griff Large, square material mounted on a frame to reflect or absorb light. Also known by its trade name, Griffolyn.

Grip Crew member whose tasks include setting up and tearing down various stands, dolly tracks, flats, flags, etc. There are several types of grips, including key grip, dolly grip, best boy grip, rigging grip, etc.

Gripology Any knowledge or information pertaining to the craft of gripping.

Griposaurus Another name for the large grip cart on wheels that contains flags, clamps, tape and many other gripology items that is kept as close to set as possible.

Groucho A cameraman asks an actor to do a "groucho" when he wants them to crouch as they walk. Inspired, of course, by the late, great Groucho Marx.

Guerrilla Filmmaking Producing a film or video without proper permits, insurance or location permission. This type of production is usually done with small crews with little or no budget who set up their cameras anywhere and start rolling.

Guide Track (G.T.) Sound track that is recorded on a set that will be used as a guide only in the editing or A.D.R. process, because of unavoidable noise such as rain, wind or mechanical sounds.

Guide Wire A small wire that is attached to an actor to guide an arrow or knife into their body to give the impression of the weapon actually hitting them.

Gyro Arm A camera device that uses a gyroscope to achieve a fluid, floating movement.

A crew works in front of a huge **Green Screen**. This allows for computer-generated effects and animation to be added in behind the images photographed on location. © 2010

Hair Light A light whose chief purpose is to accentuate an actor's hair.

Hand Crank A camera that runs on a spring wound system rather than electric power, such as a 16mm Bolex.

Hand Double Similar to a body double, a hand double is often used for a close-up on a reach-in from a character's hand to grab an object or pick it up. That way the actual actor can relax in their trailer instead of doing the shot.

Hand held A shot where the camera is carried on an operator's shoulder rather than mounted on a tripod or dolly.

Hard Equity Actual cash funds raised to produce a project. This money is put into an escrow account to ensure it is safe while the producers arrange more financing.

HDTV High Definition Television, sometimes called "High Def".

Head The unit that connects the camera to the tripod, allowing for movement and stability. See also *fluid head*.

Headroom The space between an actor's head and the top of the frame.

Hefty Herman A device that has a small platform that can be raised straight up about 20 feet with a light or a camera operator on it.

Hero A prop, car or element that is the featured item during shooting. For example, while shooting a toy commercial, many toys may be used during the day, but only one is the hero toy, or the one that is polished and perfect for filming purposes.

Hero Room A room that will actually be used while filming in a hotel, house or other building.

Hiatus A break or temporary hold on a production. Many tv series go on *hiatus* for the Christmas holidays.

Hi Hat A small camera mount screwed to a piece of wood for doing shots that are extremely low to the ground or other surface.

High Concept A movie that uses an easy to follow plot line, simple characters (often played by big stars), a huge advertising budget and lots of corporate tie-ins to ensure its success.

High Def (HD) The newest standard for video recording and playback. This format is becoming the choice for tv series, sporting events and tv movies. Also called *high definition* or *HDTV*.

HMI The HMI light was a significant advance for filming because of its ability to produce a lot of light using less power than other lights and does not produce as much heat.

H.O.D. Head of Department.

Hold the Roll Stop the action temporarily (i.e., until a car goes by or a cloud passes across the sun.)

Holding Day TO SET This term can apply to an actor or a location. A certain rate (usually less than a normal work day) is paid to be on hold. For an actor, this means they cannot go to work on another show without permission from the producers. For a location, this usually applies to weekends and other off days, or when a crew needs a set dressed and ready to go as a "cover set."

Hollywood Sweep A musical term used to describe an orchestra playing a dizzying, ascending cacophony of notes. Often used in movies to create an exalted mood or emotion.

Honeywagon The film unit trailer that contains the washrooms, A.D. box and other portable rooms.

Horror A film genre that is characterised by shocking and scaring the audience with monsters (human or other), violence or the threat of impending doom.

Horse Opera An old term for a western movie.

Hostess Tray An apparatus used to secure a camera to a car door for a shot that looks directly at a driver or passenger from the side of the car, through the car door window.

Hot A gun or explosion that is loaded and will be used in an upcoming scene. Special effects or prop people won't go "hot" on a gun or squib until the very last minute on a film production.

Hot Head Could be a name for an angry crew member, but actually refers to a remote control camera mount that is attached to the end of a crane, ceiling or other place where a cameraman can't go.

Hot Spot An overexposed portion of the frame or image.

Hot Set A set that needs to stay exactly the way it is for the continuity of shooting, either after lunch or on a later date. In other words, don't touch anything.

Hydroflex A completely waterproof camera housing unit.

Hyphenate A person who has a multitude of different talent and expertise in film production or the entertainment industry, such as a writer-director-actor, or actor-director-producer. Orson Wells could be considered a *hyphenate*, as could Clint Eastwood, Robert Redford and many others.

Photo courtesy of SpaceCam Systems Ltd. © 2010. Used with Permission.

I

IATSE International Alliance of Theatrical and Stage Employees.

IBEW International Brotherhood of Electrical Workers.

IMAX A large film format that has a high resolution and is projected onto a screen 72 feet wide and 53 feet high.

IMDb Internet Movie Database. (www.imdb.com) This website is a vast resource of information about films, directors, actors, crew and more. If you need to know who did what to whom on a movie, this is the site to find out. It has also become a verb, as in "Did you *IMDb* that person?"

Incident Light Meter An exposure meter which measures the incident light falling on a subject from all angles. Developed in the 1940's by Don Norwood, this unit remains a common tool for cinematographers.

Indie An independent film or studio. These movies quite often have a lower budget than a typical movie and less marketing muscle, but succeed because of originality, quirkiness and/or word of mouth.

Inker Animation artist who draws details and outlines with acetate ink that is applied to the cels.

Inky Dink Small, focusable studio lamp with a 250 watt bulb and a Fresnel lens.

In the Can A finished, completed project. "Yeah, that one's *in the can* now. I'm just waiting for funding on my next project."

Insert Car Vehicle used to tow the action car for moving shots. Camera and lights are usually mounted on the insert car. See also *tow shot*.

Insert Shot Brief shot of an object, such as a clock, that is "inserted" briefly into an edited segment of a film or video.

INT. Interior. A shot is always designated as INT. or EXT. in a script to help determine production requirements and costs.

ITC Intermittent Traffic Control. When shooting on location on a road or street, crews will either shut down a street completely, or use *ITC*, which allows filmmakers two or three minutes to stop traffic while doing a take.

A car-mounted **Russian Arm** with a remote camera head shoots a car chase scene. Photo courtesy of Filmotechnic Canada Ltd. © 2010. Used with Permission.

Jack Lord Camera term for a 50mm lens. (Five-0, you get it?) Book 'em, Danno.

Jib Arm A mechanical arm that has a camera at one end and a box of weights at the other, used to do sweeping shots—high or low, forward or backward. You often see jib arm shots in rock videos or in big budget Tv specials like the *Oscars*. Often the camera has a remote control hot head or power pod attached to it to do pans and tilts.

Jog To move a video or film image in short spurts during the editing or viewing process.

Juice Electricity.

Juicer A person in the electrical or lighting department.

Jump Cut A cut that appears to jump, or mismatch between shots in a scene. An example of this is a shot of a man smoking a cigarette that jumps to a shot of him without the cigarette. Unless done for a specific reason, a jump cut is considered a glaring technical imperfection, especially to sophisticated viewers that have grown up on television and film.

Junior 1) A focusable studio lamp with a Fresnel lens and 2000 watt bulb, this is one of the most common studio lighting units. 2) A small C-stand.

k Kilowatt. Used to denote the power output of a light source. (e.g., 12k, 4k, or 2k)

Keeper A shot or take that will most likely be used in a film. If a shot is called a "keeper" by a director, it usually means that no additional takes will be required.

Kelvin A measurement of colour temperature.

Key Grip Person in charge of the grip department responsible for overseeing dolly track placement, lighting diffusion and other grip tasks.

Key Light Main light used to illuminate a set.

Kicker 1) A light source positioned behind and to the side of a subject, usually on the side opposite the key light. It is used to separate foreground objects from the background. 2) A mortar explosion that is intended to move an object physically during a take.

Kill To stop, turn off or otherwise get rid of a light, sound or vehicle. "Kill the pickup truck now!"

Kinetoscope One of the first cameras used for capturing motion pictures, built by Thomas Edison in the 1890's.

Knuckle Round metal clamp used in conjunction with C-stands, baby plates, gobo arms, etc.

Lamp Op A *lamp operator* is part of the electrics crew, and is often assigned to setting up and monitoring one or more lights on a set.

Lavalier (lav) See *wire*.

Leader A segment, usually at the beginning of a videotape or film that is just a black screen with no sound.

Letterbox A method of showing a feature film widescreen image on television, by making the picture smaller and putting black areas on the top and bottom of the screen.

Library Shot See *stock footage*.

Lighting Department That part of the crew responsible for all lighting and electricity requirements for a set. Also called *electrics* or *sparks*.

Limbo This term refers to the absence of reference. A scene is shot in limbo when there is no reference to the surrounding environment, like one shot against total black.

Limpet Mount Named after the gastropod creature of the same name, this is a camera mount that can stick onto any flat surface, such as a car hood.

Linear Editing The old-fashioned way of editing, in one continuous line from beginning to end. See also *non-linear editing*.

Line Producer Producer in charge of the actual finances and day to day supervision of spending and costs on a film production.

Liner A back light, similar to a kicker but on the same side as a key light.

Lipstick camera An extremely small camera that can be concealed on an actor or on a set. Also called a *bullet cam* due to its small, tube-like shape, and a *helmet cam* because it can be mounted on one.

Lip Synch When an actor synchronises his mouth and lip movements to an audio playback.

Live Prop A slang term for an extra or background performer.

Location TO SET Place of filming that is not on a studio lot or sound-stage.

Location Fee TO SET A fee paid to the owner of a location that is used in the production of a film.

Location Manager (L.M.) TO SET Person in charge of finding locations to the satisfaction of the director (whether by existing files or scouting), striking deals with property owners, and ensuring a minimum of damage occurs to locations while shooting takes place. They also deal with permits, insurance and abnormal locations requests from various department heads, like blowing up a bus on a major city bridge or shooting late at night in residential neighbourhoods.

Location Scout Person who finds and photographs possible locations under the supervision of the location manager.

Lock it up Prevent any activity or disruption that could interfere with the shot. Generally applies to pedestrians, vehicle traffic and noise in general.

Logline A brief one or two-sentence synopsis of a film or tv program.

Long Lens A telephoto or zoom lens that is 100mm or larger.

Looping The act of re-recording an actor's lines in a studio while they match their voice to the screen, often at great expense to the production and sometimes months from when the scene was originally shot.

Losing the light A common problem for filmmakers shooting outside or on location when the natural light from the sun is quickly going away.

L.S. Long Shot.

M

M & E Music and effects. When doing the final sound mix for a film, all of the sounds are broken down into three categories: dialogue, music and effects. When dubbing for a foreign language, the M&E tracks can be easily seperated from the dialogue tracks.

MacGuffin The catalyst for action or a sequence of events in a Hitchcock movie. A MacGuffin is usually a thing that has nothing to do with the characters or building of suspense, but it is what drives the plot along. (For example, the uranium ore in *Notorious* or the secret airplane plans in *The 39 Steps.*)

Mae West Shot A shot that frames an actor from the top of their head to just below their chest.

Magazine The canister that holds the film in a motion picture camera. Also called a *mag.*

Magic Arm Leg Three legged stand used by grips for small, confined spaces.

Magic Hour That part of the day just before sunset when everything is bathed in a golden light.

Mag Stock Short for *magnetic stock.* Film stock used for sound tracks, usually dubbed from a Nagra or DAT machine, so it may be synchronised to the visual portion of a film. Also referred to as *mag*.

Main Unit The main film crew (including trucks and equipment) that is responsible for *principal photography.* A main unit crew will shoot the majority of the scenes for any given production including those with the lead actors. The *2nd Unit,* on the other hand, will usually shoot establishing, connecting and action segments with photo or stunt doubles in place of the lead actors. See also *splinter unit.*

Maquette Small doll or puppet used by special effects people.

Mark 1) When a camera assistant holds the slate in front of the lens before a take, he calls out "mark" just before he claps the sticks together. 2) A tape or chalk mark used so an actor can hit a specific spot during a take.

Martini Shot See *window shot.*

Married When a film's audio and visual portions are put together, the result is called a *married print.*

Mask A blocking device attached to the front of the camera. This technique is often used to give the impression that someone is looking through a telescope or binoculars.

Master Shot A wide or main shot of a scene which is inserted or supplemented with other camera shots in the editing room.

Match When a key position on a film is taken by someone from out of the country, unions require a "match" for that person in the same category. For instance, if a sound effects recordist is brought to Canada from L.A., a *match mixer* is hired to assist them and be their "shadow" for the duration of the time they are there.

Match Dissolve A dissolve in which two images that are similar in size and balance dissolve into each other.

Matte A mask used on the camera or optical printer to prevent certain areas from being exposed, which are used later to insert other backgrounds.

Matte Box A box-like device that fits at the end of a camera lens to protect it from light reflections and provides a receptacle for filters and special effects mattes.

Matte Painting A painting that can be used to simulate a real background, so that moving images may be overlaid on top of it.

Maquette Can also refer to small mock-ups or models of buildings, etc.

M.C.U. Medium close-up.

Meat Axe An adjustable device that clamps onto catwalks to mount lights, etc.

Meat Puppet Slang term for a stunt performer.

Method Acting An acting or performance style that requires total commitment on the part of the actor to literally become whatever physical or mental state their character is in. If their character is tired, they stay up for 24 hours, if they're hungry, they don't eat for three days. This approach to acting was created and refined in New York, through acting mentor Stanislavsky.

Mickey Mousing Background music that takes its cue directly from the action on the screen, mimicking its every move. This term comes from the early cartoons such as Mickey Mouse, and the technique was later used heavily in Bugs Bunny and other shows.

Mickey Rooney A very slow and short dolly move, i.e. "a little creep."

Miller's Triangle A theoretical triangle which represents green, blue and red, and is applied to black and white photography. The idea is that as you add a filter of one of the colours it diminishes that hue and brings up the others.

Miniature A small model replica of a building or vehicle that is doubling as the real thing in a movie.

Mini Move TO SET A move of only the core production vehicles, not the entire unit, while filming on location.

Mirror Shot A shot that looks into a mirror.

Mise-en-scene The complete, visual presentation of a scene, with the combined elements of lighting, costumes, sets, actors, etc.

Mo See *day mo*.

Mo Ho Slang term for a motorhome, which is often used on tv commercial shoots as the production office, makeup/wardrobe trailer and film crew headquarters.

M.O.L. "Mit Out Light," is a derivation of M.O.S., and refers to a scene requiring no artificial light.

Mo-Cap Short for "motion capture," a technique used for animation and gaming where a live human wears a suit that has motion sensors in it and stands in front of a blue or green screen and moves around. This motion is then transferred into the digital domain for more realistic movement of characters.

Mockumentary A movie that appears to be a documentary but is actually scripted and played by professional actors. One of the most successful and hilarious mockumentaries (or rockumentaries) is Rob Reiner's spoof of the rock music business *Spinal Tap*.

Mombo Combo An extremely heavy-duty stand used by grips that can extend high into the air.

Money The main star. To 'shoot for the money' is to get the star in the shot. Clint Eastwood is known to use this phrase.

Montage From the French word *monter* (literally, "to mount"), this is a sequence of shots, or a way of utilising editing to create a certain effect. Russian film great Sergei Eisenstein was one of the first filmmakers to really explore the possibilities of montage in the early part of this century.

Mook A totally green or low on the totem pole crew member.

Morph To have one object visually transform into another object through the use of a computer.

M.O.S. A camera shot that requires no sound to be recorded. From the early German directors' use of the phrase, "mit out sound."

Motion Control A remote controlled system that can be programmed with precise camera moves so they can be repeated exactly the same every time. This can be extremely effective for duplicating a character in the same shot with camera moves, and for working with miniatures, stop motion and composite elements.

Moviola A film projection device used to view film during the editing process.

M.O.W. Movie of the Week. Also called a *tv movie*.

M.P. Meal Penalty. One good thing about most film unions is that they make sure crew members have to get a meal after working a certain number of hours or be paid a penalty if they go past the scheduled time.

Murmur Crowd background noise that is quiet and indiscernible. See also *walla* and *babble*.

Music Supervisor The person who selects and secures music for a production and negotiates licensing rights and usage.

NABET National Association of Broadcast Employees and Technicians.

Nagra Swiss made analogue tape recorder, used almost exclusively in the past to record dialogue, sound and sound effects on a film production. Now almost everything is recorded digitally.

Narration Spoken-word recording or commentary that is layered onto a visual image. Narration is often used in documentaries, nature films and news programs. See also *voice-over*.

Narrative Film A film that tells a story in a straightforward way, from beginning to end.

NC-17 A film that is rated as not appropriate for viewers under the age of 17, due to elements of sex, violence, drug use or deviant behaviour within the film.

ND Filter Colourless filter that reduces the amount of light entering a camera lens. *ND* stands for neutral density.

N.D. Nondescript. Usually applies to a generic car or extra needed for a scene. (i.e. "Bring me five ND people and one ND car for this shot")

Negative Cutter The negative cutter takes the negative of a movie and conforms, or matches, it to the final cut of the film as decided by the director, editor, producer and others. Final prints of the film are created from this conformed negative.

Neorealism A style of filmmaking which was developed and popularised in post WWII Italy, and features stories of the poor and working class set in real locations, often with "found" or untrained actors. Films such as *Bicycle Thief* and *La Strada* are examples of Italian Neorealism.

N.F.B. The National Film Board of Canada.

Camera on Sticks (Tripod)
Photo by: Joseph MacKinnon © 2010. Used with permission.

New Hollywood The era of American filmmaking that started in 1969 with *Easy Rider*, a counter culture "indie" that cost $340,000 to produce and ended up earning over $19 million. The group includes innovative filmmakers Francis Ford Coppola, Martin Scorcese, Steven Spielberg, George Lucas, Peter Bogdanovich, Hal Ashby, Robert Towne, Paul Schrader et al.

N.G. No good.

N.F.G. No #$%@*! good.

Non-Linear Editing A modern method of editing that utilises computer workstations to edit a film or video. Footage may be stored in the computer and assembled in any order. If the resulting edits are not quite right , they can be stored in the memory on the computer and shuffled around very easily.

Bird's Eye View
Photo by: Joseph MacKinnon © 2010. Used with permission.

Oater Another word for a western movie.

Obie Light A small light mounted on the camera to light up an actor's eyes. It was originally designed by cinematographer Lucien Ballard for his actress-wife, Merle Oberon. See also *eyelight*.

Off Line Editing Basically a rough edit that uses safe "work copies" of the audio and visual material of a film before a final cut is made with the master film stock. A computer is generally used to keep track of where the cuts occur, called an Edit Decision List, or EDL.

One-er A shot that may be finished off with only one camera set-up.

One Liner 1) A short joke from a comedian. 2) A preproduction schedule that breaks each scene down into one line that describes it, such as "John tells Jackie that he doesn't have the rent money." It also includes scene numbers, set, actors needed, etc.

On Line Editing When editing is done using the original footage for a final master edit of the movie or video. When completed, the final product will be of "broadcast quality," ready to be copied and distributed to waiting audiences.

On Spec To offer your services on a project without being paid until the project gets off the ground or makes money at some point down the road. This kind of work is speculative because there is no guarantee that you will be ever paid.

On the Clock When a crew is officially being paid for their services, like at the beginning of a day or after lunch.

On the Day When we actually roll the cameras, as in, "O.K., *on the day* we'll drive the car through this wall and out onto the street."

On the Move A phrase used on a set when the crew is changing set-ups or moving to a different location.

Op Short for *operator*, as in camera op, or light op.

Optical An effect that uses an optical print to add other layers onto the film.

Optical Printer A special printer that can combine two or more images for special effects, titles, superimpositions, split screen or a myriad of other invaluable photographic effects not possible with a normal film image.

Option A script term. A studio may purchase the rights to a script as an *option*. In other words they will pay the screenwriter for the "option" of producing it someday, or for a set time period (anywhere from 6 months to two years). Many times an optioned script will stay on the shelf for months if not years, at which point the contract will lapse and it goes back to the writer or copyright owner.

O.S. Off-screen. In a script, a line of dialogue or action that is not seen by the camera, but affects the action that is on-screen.

Oscar The golden statue award given out by the Academy of Motion Picture Arts and Sciences. Also called an *Academy Award.* The statue got its famous nickname when a production seamstress said it reminded her of her "Uncle Oscar." The first Academy Awards were given out in May of 1929.

Outline A rough sketch of a script.

Out-take A shot that is not used in the final show.

Overkeeper Device that allows a camera to slide horizontally while attached to a dolly mount.

Overlap Sound or image that is laid on top of another for editing purposes.

Over Scale When a performer or crew member becomes quite established in the industry, they often negotiate a higher rate of pay than what is the "scale" rate for that position. See also *scale.*

Over the Shoulder (OTS) A shot often used when two people are having a conversation in a film. It incorporates part of the listener's shoulder while framing the speaker, to give the impression of being there.

P

P.A. 1) Production assistant. Person employed to help out a film production in so many ways it would be impossible to list them all here. Duties could include crowd control, security, clean-up, public relations, traffic control, keeping crew members quiet, and many other tasks. 2) Public address. An audio system consisting of a microphone, amplifier and speakers.

P & A Prints and advertising. This is the marketing segment of the distribution phase of a movie that includes posters and ads for billboards, bus stops, newspapers, magazines, the internet and television

Pan 1) A camera movement from left to right, or vice versa. 2) When a critic gives a bad review of a movie.

Pancake A small, thin rectangular box used for elevating pieces of gear.

Pass-bys People or vehicles that pass through the frame to create a feeling of realism.

PAR Parabolic Aluminised Reflector. A light that has a self-contained reflector and lens.

Parallel Editing A technique developed by D.W. Griffiths that uses direct cutting between two simultaneously occurring scenes to heighten suspense or climactic excitement.

Pattern Budget On a tv series, each head of department provides a budget before the series starts that is an estimate of what they think each episode will cost for them.

Pay or Play Deal An agreement between a production company and a high-level crew member, director or actor that guarantees that person will be paid out for the entire run of the show even if the show stops filming or is cancelled for any reason.

Peewee 1) Small camera dolly. 2) A small light.

Pepper Small (100w) light used to illuminate tiny nooks" and crannies

Per Diem Money paid daily to crew members for meals and expenses while shooting out of town.

Period Piece A movie that is set in a previous or bygone time period, usually with elaborate sets, costumes, props and locations. *Amadeus* and *Dangerous Liasons* are good examples of this type of film. Sometimes called a *costume drama.*

Petty Cash (PC) Money used by a production or a crew member to pay for expenses that are generally below $200, such as fuel, meals, parking as well as props, set dec and wardrobe purchases. Always remember to ask for a *PC Advance* when you start a show, so you won't have to dip into your own bank account.

Pick-Up Shot A shot that must be added to the schedule because there is something missing that needs to be "picked up" before the show wraps.

Picture Car Car or vehicle that is used in a film.

Photo Double A person who dresses and has their makeup and hair done to look exactly like a lead cast member. A photo double is often used for 2nd Unit shots where the camera is on such a long lens that you really can't see for sure who it is anyway.

Picture's Up When rehearsals are over, and the crew is getting ready to roll right away.

Pitch To present a script concept or actor/writer/director package in verbal form to a producer or financier. It basically boils down to somebody trying to convince someone else to put money into a project.

Pilot The first program in a television series, generally a two-hour, made-for-tv movie.

Plate Shot A fixed shot, usually done on location, which will be augmented with visual effects/CGI elements during the editing phase.

Playback Sound or visuals that are "played back" during a take, such as music for rock videos or a tv segment that is part of the shot.

Pop A close up shot which does not necessarily cover the entire scene. "We can probably cover this scene with a master shot and a couple of *pops*."

Pork chop A small board that attaches to dollies for the camera operator to stand on. Named because of its strange shape resembling a pork product.

Poor Man's Process (PMP) A way of creating the illusion of movement for an interior scene in a car by shaking it up and down and flashing lights and shadows across it.

Post Production The part of a production that includes the editing and finishing aspects of a production, after all of the scenes have been shot. May be subdivided into audio and visual editing, packaging, distribution, etc.

POV Point of View. Shot that assumes the character's line of vision in a scene. "Let's turn it around now and get his *POV* of the room."

Practical Anything that is operational on a set, like a table lamp or a kitchen sink.

Premiere The first showing of a movie in public, often with huge hype and fanfare, and attended by famous people. Often characterised by stars arriving by limousines and a red carpet walk to the theatre.

Pre-Production Everything that must be taken care of before shooting starts, including casting, hiring of department heads, shooting schedule, script breakdown, scouting and securing locations, securing financing and many other details. Usually, the more time spent and effort spent in pre-production, the more smoothly the production will go.

Pretties Slang for the Hair, Make-up and Wardrobe departments. Sometimes used to refer to the trucks that are used by these departments.

Previz Pre-visualisation. A 3 dimensional "storyboard" of a shot or sequence of shots in a virtual or animated setting. Directors use previz as a creative tool to help them pre-visualise how a shot or edited scene will look before they actually film it, particularly action scenes or those that are combined with CG elements. Also called *pre-viz* or *3-D storyboarding.*

Primacord Highly explosive cord of various grains used by the special effects crew to blow things up.

Primes The lenses most used and needed by a camera crew.

Principal A main actor or character in a show. Not to be confused with a bit part actor or, heaven forbid, an extra.

Principal Photography The main bulk of filming for a movie. The start of principal photography is when all of the crew and main actors are present, and it ends when they are finished. Sometimes portions of a movie are shot before and after principal photography, such as plate shots, establishing shots, close-ups, insert shots and 2nd unit shots.

Process Shot A technique of filming that combines live action with a projected background. This technique was used a lot in the old days when shooting actors in a car, with a moving background projected on a screen behind the car.

Producer Person who oversees all aspects of a production at every stage along the way. The producer locks in the financing for each project, as well as being involved in creative decisions such as script rewrites, who will be cast in the movie, and how the film will be distributed.

Production Co-ordinator (P.C.) Person who runs the production office under the guidelines of the production manager. Tasks may include organising equipment rentals, customs brokers, hotel rooms for actors and directors, relaying messages to and from set, and a myriad of other duties, many of which are assigned to the assistant production co-ordinator or the office P.A.

Production Designer (P.D.) Person who, in conjunction with the art director, is responsible for the entire visual look of a film, and makes decisions about set decoration, props, make-up and wardrobe in the pre-production phase and supervises these elements during shooting.

Production Manager (P.M.) Person who ensures the production runs smoothly and as planned, always keeping a close eye on budget and unnecessary expenses, such as time delays.

A **Picture Vehicle** adds realism when filming on location. © 2010

Production Office The office space that is the central hub of activity during prep, shoot and wrap for a production. The office is usually a large, open "bullpen" area that will have room for the Production Co-ordinator, Assistants and Office P.A.'s. Other offices are usually connected or close to this main office that are used by key crew and departments such as Locations, A.D.'s, Transport, PM, Producers, Accounting and the Art Department.

Production Report A daily report of what scenes were shot, how much film was shot, in and out times for all crew members and actors, and comments on special circumstances or problems that may have delayed the production. Also called a DPR or *daily production report*.

Production Schedule A detailed breakdown of a film's shooting schedule that outlines each day of production including info about which scenes will be shot on which days, and which actors, props and locations are required for those days.

Product Placement To prominently feature or display a product such as a can of soda in a film or tv show. Large sums of money have been paid by advertisers to film companies to show famous actors using their products on camera.

Prop 1) Slang for *property*. Any object used by an actor in a film. 2) Property: A story or script (usually owned by a studio) that is waiting to be made into a movie.

Prop Buyer Person employed, under the supervision of the propmaster, to acquire props to be used in a film.

Property Master Usually called a propmaster, this is the person in charge of acquiring props as required by the script and overseeing their use during a production. Propmasters and their assistants are almost always firearms technicians, trained in the safe use of guns and ammunition.

Pull Focus See *rack*.

Pull the plug To halt the production of a film, whether it is just for the current filming day because of a curfew, or to stop the entire show from going on due to a lack of funds. "At eleven o'clock we have to *pull the plug* for the night."

Pump Cup A small suction cup that is "pumped" to hold the cup to a wall, ceiling or other flat surface to attach lights, flags, etc.

Push 1) When a shooting schedule is moved ahead for whatever reason. 2) Overdeveloping film in the lab to compensate for low lighting conditions.

Pyrotechnics The area of the special effects department that deals with controlled fire, flames and explosions. Sometimes shortened to *pyro*.

P.Z.M. Pressure zone microphone. A flat microphone that is usually taped to a piece of plexiglass to record extremely loud sounds such as gunblasts and explosions.

Quartz Lamp A specific type of lamp that uses a quartz filament for a constant colour temperature.

Quick Study When an actor reads a specific portion of a script in a hurried fashion to get the gist of a scene.

On Location Shoot © 2010

R

Rack When a camera changes, or "pulls" focus from one object to another during a shot. Also known as a *pull focus*, or *rack focus*.

Rainbow Script The first draft of a script is always on white paper. As each revision is done prior to shooting, new script changes are added to the existing script in different colors each step along the way. By the time the script is in its final form it often has every color of the rainbow in it.

Rain Towers Huge metal tube towers set up by the FX dept. to simulate rain on a set, from a slight drizzle to a torrential downpour.

Rake A camera or lighting angle that is neither head-on nor a profile, but rather a diagonal.

Ramp To speed up or slow down a moving image. Sometimes a ramp in/out of freeze is an effective attention grabber in a film.

Ramping An editing term that refers to the speeding up or slowing down of a particular shot.

Raw Footage Unedited film footage.

Raw Stock Unexposed film stock.

Rear Screen Projection A method of projecting an image onto an opaque screen meant to be played behind the subject that is being filmed. This technique was used extensively in the 50's and 60's whenever an actor was driving a car. The scene was usually filmed on a sound stage with a rear screen projection of a moving background playing behind the car, giving the illusion of movement. Although it looked a little cheesy back then, rear screen technology has vastly improved since then and is still in use today. See also *process shot*.

Recci Short for *reconnaissance*. This comes from the British filmmaking world. "Let's go for a *recci*," means to go for a location scout or survey.

Redhead A small light named for its red casing.

Red One A powerful and affordable high-resolution HD camera that is used for many tv series and independent features.

Release Print The print of a film or video that is released for distribution to tv stations or movie theatres.

Remote Head A camera head that can perform tilts, pans, zooms and focusing from a remote control unit. These heads are often used at the end of a long crane or boom where the camera operator and focus puller can't reach. Also called a *hot head* or *flight head*.

Render A computer process that finalises an edit, especially those with visual effects, compositing or CGI elements. Most people take a break at this time to go for a smoke or coffee break while the computer "crunches" the data.

Re-recording Mixer The person who prepares the dialogue, effects and music tracks and supervises the final sound mix for a movie or television show. They call it re-recording because the three sound elements have already been recorded and they are to be re-recorded onto the final track.

Reset After a take has been done, the 1st A.D. will often call for a reset to bring actors, vehicles and extras back to their original positions for another take. Also called *first positions, back to one, going again* or *number ones.*

Residuals Money paid to a performer or crew member every time the production is broadcast, in addition to the original amount they were paid. TV commercials and series can be quite lucrative to anyone who has residuals built into their contract for a production.

Reverse Angle To flip the camera around 180 degrees to shoot the reverse of what it was previously filming.

Rider Anything added onto an actor or producer or director's contract that is a special requirement or need that must be met. For example, you could have a *rider* on your contract that says you must have fresh-squeezed organic guava juice ready for you when you arrive on set each day.

Ripple Dissolve Popularised by Wayne and Garth in *Wayne's World*, the *ripple dissolve* is a blending of two images with a ripple effect, often denoting a transition into a dream or flashback.

Risk Performance When an actor performs next to a stunt person he is compensated for the amount of risk involved in doing so. Sometimes called *stunt pay* or *stunt adjustment*.

Rocker See *gimbal*.

Rolling When you hear this word on a set, it means that the camera, and usually sound, are running. "We're rolling ... Speed!...Scene four take twelve 'A' only, mark...And, action!"

Room Tone The sound or tone of a specific room or location that the location sound mixer records without any noise or talking. This is an important element to have for the sound mixing process to give the track added sonic dimension and realism. Also called *ambient sound*.

Rotoscoping A form of animation that traces over a moving image one frame at a time. This technique was created early in the 20th century, but in today's digital world it is used for frame-by-frame manipulation of shots, digital painting, removing unwanted elements or creating animated mattes.

Rough Cut A temporary edit of a film or video with some rough edges that are to be worked out.

Rumble Pot A device used for creating a low lying fog on movie sets. The container boils water, and then a basket full of crushed dry ice is lowered into the water, creating a low ground fog cloud. The pot makes a lot of rumbling, bubbling sounds, hence its name.

Rushes See *dailies*.

Russian Arm 3 The *Russian Arm* is a remotely operated gyro-stabilised camera crane system that keeps the camera steady while moving at high speeds and across bumpy terrain. The lightweight design allows the crane to be mounted on the roof of almost any camera car, boat, train or other mobile platform. Often used for car commercials and action scenes when shooting car to car, people on horseback or any other moving objects.

Russian Arm
Photo courtesy of Filmotechnic Canada Ltd. © 2010. Used with Permission.

S

S.A.G.  Screen Actors Guild. (U.S.)

Saddle Bags A type of sandbag that has a handle in the middle with two sacks of sand on each side.

Sandbag A small sack of canvas or leather filled with sand which anchors stands and sets from falling over, and is also used as a mark for actors or vehicles.

Scale A set rate of pay for a writer, performer or crew member, as determined by their union or guild.

Scene A segment of a film or tv show that is composed of a series of shots, and usually takes place in one time and place

Scooch To move an object or actor. Similar to "cheat."

Scoop A studio lamp with a soft, wide throw of 500 to 2000 watts.

Score 1) Musical composition that is layered into the soundtrack of a film. 2) Actual written piece of music that is used by musicians to play the music.

Scout To physically go and look at potential locations for a project. See also *location scout*.

Screenplay A full length script for a movie.

Screenwriter The person who is credited with writing an original screenplay or adaptation from a book or story.

Screwball Comedy A comedy genre that has a zany plot line or outrageous characters that get mixed up in a series of unusual and funny circumstances. This type of comedy has its origins in, and is similar to a comedy of errors, popular in Shakespeare's time.

Scrim Round stainless steel screens that go in front of lights to reduce the intensity of the brightness.

Script Supervisor The person responsible for keeping track of the take and roll numbers, camera and sound reloads, script revisions, how long each take lasts, scene numbers, slate numbers, prompting the actor(s) when they forget their lines, and making sure that continuity is upheld between takes and different angles. Also called a *continuity person*.

Second Assistant Director (2nd A.D.) The person responsible for preparing the call sheet in consultation with the 1st A.D., arranging for pick-ups and drop-offs of actors and for calling in to the production office to alert them on the progress of the shooting day (first shot times, meal penalties, etc.).

Second Meal When a crew works a certain amount of hours past lunch, a second meal is prepared or ordered for the crew.

Second Team See *stand-in*.

Second Unit A separate, smaller crew on a production that is responsible for getting establishing shots, or any shots that were not achieved with the main unit.

S.E.G. Screen Extras Guild. (U.S.)

Segue A musical or visual cue that carries from one transition to the next without interruption.(pronounced *seg-way*)

Sensitive Location A location such as a park or an expensive home where extra care must be taken not to damage or destroy walls, trees, furniture, etc.

Set The place, either on location or in a studio, where a tv show or movie is filmed.

Set Dec Short for Set Decoration, this is the department responsible for how a set looks during a shot.

Set Dresser Person who "dresses the set" with decorations, artwork, rugs, etc. Sometimes called an on-set dresser, this person must supervise the continuity of sets under the supervision of the set decorator or art director.

Shark Fins Thin metal objects shaped like shark fins that are used by the sound mixer as antennae for their wireless microphones.

Shockumentary A style of documentary program that uses shocking images or subject matter as a main way of telling the story.

Shooting ratio A mathematical ratio of how much film was shot versus how much is used in the final program. The smaller the ratio (i.e. 4:1 or 3:1) the more economical the shoot.

Shooting Schedule A complete schedule of all of the scenes from a production and on which day they are slated to be shot.

Shooting Script A script that has been broken into scene numbers. This is the script that will actually be referred to during prep and filming. See also *rainbow script* and *story script*.

Shop To actively push a new project or series in order to get it sold or produced. This is similar in many ways to a musician or band *shopping* their music demo to various record labels to get a deal.

Shop Steward Person that represents the crew from a union perspective, ensuring that people receive proper turn-around, overtime and working conditions. This person is usually a crew member on the show.

Short A film or video presentation that is less than one hour long. Also called a *short film*.

Short Ends Unexposed pieces of film that are donated by professional, big-budget productions to beginning or independent filmmakers to use in their films.

Shotgun Mic A long, cylindrical directional microphone that is used for recording distant sounds.

Shot listing Days before a shoot begins a director will sit down with his DP and 1st AD and go through the various shots (handheld, tripod, dolly, crane, etc.) he or she will use to film each scene.

Sides A small printout of the pages from the script that are to be "shot" on each day. Actors, directors and crew often carry these around with them to refer to when needed.

Sight Line The direction an actor is looking during a shot. It can be very important to keep an actor's sightline clear to ensure he or she can concentrate properly. Also called an *eyeline*.

Sky Pans Non-focusable 5k lights that are used to illuminate sets or translights. These are large lights that are much thinner than a typical 5k or 10k light, but give out a large wash of light.

Slapstick A style of comedy that involves pies in the face, people falling and tripping and other physical humour.

Slasher A style of horror movie that features people being stabbed, sliced and hacked to pieces, usually with lots of fake blood spurting everywhere.

Slate Small blackboard with spaces for the title of the production, the scene number, the take number, the cameraman's name and the name of the production company producing the film. When both the camera and tape recorder are running at speed, the director instructs the assistant to "mark it," or "slate it," with a clap of the two pieces of board, before calling "action." Used to synchronise the sound with the picture when editing later on. See also *clapper*.

Slate-in When auditioning before a camera, an actor is expected to give his or her name, age, agent's name and other important details so they may be referred to later.

Sleeper A movie released by the studios that is not expected to do really well.

Slow Motion (Slow Mo) A shot that moves slower than "real" time. This type of shot is used to build suspense or draw our attention to something or someone in a scene. Slo-mo is often achieved by shooting with the film going through the camera at a faster rate than the usual 24fps. When played back at normal speed, it makes everything appear to move slower. These days, slow motion effects can also be achieved through digital manipulation.

Slug A piece of film which will be replaced at a later date that is inserted in a work print.

Slush Truck Truck used to haul miscellaneous items such as chairs, tables, heaters, fans and tarps. Also called a *gak truck*.

Smotherage To over shoot, or get too much coverage for a scene.

SMPTE Society of Motion Picture and Television Engineers. This is also the name given to a type of time code striped onto video tape for syncing purposes.

Snoot Funnel shaped device attached to lamps instead of barn doors for a more precise light beam.

Snot Sticky putty used by set dec and grips to temporarily hold various items in place.

Snow Blankets Large, white "blankets" of material used to cover large areas of a set or location in order to make it look covered in snow.

S.O.C. Silent On Camera. When an actor is used in a scene more prominently than a typical extra but doesn't have any spoken lines, a "silent on camera" credit and wage upgrade is given to that person. This term is used mostly for commercials.

Soft Focus A method of filming that purposely leaves part or all of the frame out of focus to achieve a "soft" effect on the subject. This can be achieved in a number of different ways, including filters, Vaseline on a piece of glass over the lens, or a focusing of the lens itself.

Soft Money The portion of a film's budget that comes in the form of tax breaks or other government subsidies or incentives. Also called *soft equity*.

Sotto When an actor speaks quietly or under their breath, like a whisper. Sometimes they may be talking to another character or to themselves so other characters do not hear them. This is mostly used in theatre, where the term originated.

Soubrette An actress playing a young, flirtatious woman.

Sound Mixer The person in charge of recording all of the sound on a movie set, including dialog, sound effects and room tone, as well as alerting the director as to what will and will not be a usable sound take during a shot.

Sound Optical The use of sound to create a layered effect in the editing process, much like an optical effect would do for a visual image. For example, a soundtrack that continues from one scene to the next, even though the visual image has changed is called a *sound optical*.

Sound Stage A studio where scenes involving dialogue are filmed.

Source Music Music in a film or video that comes from something seen or implied onscreen, such as a radio, tape or CD player, jukebox or musician. Does not apply to background or theme music that is simply added to the soundtrack. Also called *actual music.*

SpaceCam A gyro-stabilising device that is attached to a helicopter, plane or blimp for incredibly smooth shots. Used extensively in movies such as the *Lord of the Rings* trilogy. See also *Wescam.*

SPFX See *special effects.*

Spaghetti with pizza on the side Slang term for a dolly track with a dolly set on top of it (the operator's chair is round).

Sparks Slang term for someone in the electrics or lighting department.

Sparrow Plate A small, narrow plate used by grips to mount flags, lights or other devices.

Speaking Part When an actor has specific lines to say in a film or tv show. An actor may also have a non-speaking part when they are characters in the show but don't say anything.

Spec Script A script that is written on the speculation that someone may purchase it at some point. Not to be confused with a paid contract or assignment. Also called *on spec.*

Special Effects The department that deals with explosions, squibs, blood packets, rain, snow, wind, fog and many other pyrotechnic and visual effects. Also known as *SPFX* or *FX.*

Special Effects Co-Ordinator The person in charge of the FX department. The co-ordinator must be extremely knowledgeable about explosives, rigging and safety as he or she often has to deal with dangerous circumstances and unpredictability.

Speed Word yelled out by the sound mixer when his tape recorder is rolling. This term dates back to the old studio days when the crew literally had to get an electrical charge built up to a certain rate before they could power the cameras.

Spider Three strips of plastic or metal that spread out the legs of a tripod. Also called a *spreader*.

Spider Cam A remote-controlled camera dolly that can be combined with a gyro head for extremely smooth dolly shots while booming up or down, panning and tilting.

Spin Off A television show or movie that comes from another show. For instance, the popular tv series *Frasier* is a *spin off* of the immensely successful *Cheers!*

Splinter Unit Part of the main unit of a production that breaks away to do other setups and shots at a different location. Also called a *swing unit*.

Split Screen A technique used to divide a scene into multiple images, so an actor may play a dual role on the same screen, or to give the impression that an actor is in the same shot as a dangerous animal.

Spot A tv or radio commercial. A spot can be also referred to as :15, :30, or :60 to denote a fifteen, thirty or sixty second commercial.

Spot Meter A device used by cinematographers that measures reflective light within a narrow field of view.

Spotting When doing the editing or sound editing on a film, a spotting session is done to make notes on what will be required in the post production process (such as possible problems with dialog or missing shots).

Squib A small explosive charge that is planted and camouflaged on an area where a gunshot is supposed to hit. A squib is generally wired or connected to a remote control device and then discharged at the appropriate time by a special effects person.

Stealing the shot To shoot a scene or take without permits or any kind of lockup. Sophia Coppola used this technique in Tokyo, Japan to great success in her Oscar-winning film, *Lost in Translation*. See also *guerilla filmmaking*.

Step Deal When a film gets an investor to put up a portion of the money for a film, then the producer can take that as one "step" towards getting all of the financing they need to make the film. Sometimes called a *yellow light*.

Stinger Slang for an a/c power extension cord. Also simply called *A/C*.

Studio 1) A film company such as New Line, Paramount or Dreamworks that produces a large number of films or tv programs. 2) The place where a film or musical performance is filmed or recorded. See also *soundstage*.

S.S.E. Special Skills Extra. If an extra is required to do something in a scene that requires a skill such as playing an instrument or riding a bike, an upgrade is given to them.

Stand-by Be prepared for shooting—everything is in place and the 1st A.D. has their hand on the trigger finger.

Standby Painter The person who is in charge of all painting and spray bombing on a movie set. Whether it is touch ups of furniture or scenery or even the grass, the standby painter must be ready to colour our world at an instant's notice.

Stand-in A person who stands in the place of the principal actors while the cameras and lights are set up. This gives the actors a chance to take a break, practise their lines or graze at craft service. Also referred to as *second team*.

Starlight A truck that has its own generator, light and crane to provide night lighting for exterior shots.

Start Pack Bundle of papers that must be filled out by cast and crew members when beginning work on a film production. The start pack includes a tax form, deal memo, safety guidelines, start slip and many other bureaucratic forms.

Starwagon Large trailer that houses temporary rooms for actors while filming on location.

Steadicam Camera stabilising device invented in 1974 by Garret Brown that hooks up to the operator's body with a harness. It allows for moving the camera without using dollies or cranes, giving a smooth flowing image throughout a scene (i.e. running up stairs, going in and out of elevators.) Often used as a POV camera.

Sticks 1) Slang term for a tripod. 2) Slang term for the clapper, or clapboard.

Stills As opposed to moving pictures, stills are photographs taken for promotional material and publications.

Still Photographer Person responsible for taking pictures of actors and sets during filming.

Stipple The technique used by makeup artists to apply facial hair on actors such as moustaches and beards.

Stock Footage Archived footage that is stored and sold to filmmakers. Stock footage may included shots of cityscapes, H-bomb explosions, volcanoes, or other shots that may be hard to get or costly to reproduce.

Stop-Motion A form of animation which uses small puppets shot one painstaking frame at a time to achieve the look of fluid motion when projected at the standard 24 frames per second.

Storyboard Sequence of drawings in comic book format that is assembled before attempting a shot for real, so the director and his or her crew are sure of what and how they are going to shoot.

Story Script The version of a script that is in its original format from the writer(s). This "virgin" or "white" script does not contain any scene numbers.

Strike To disassemble or take down a set after filming is completed.

Stunt Any type of action during a scene that involves the possibility of an actor being hurt, such as fighting, falling from a building or jumping from a moving car.

Stunt Adjustment An extra amount of cash given to a stunt person depending on the severity of a stunt. Some stunt people have received several thousands of dollars for one stunt because they risked their lives doing it.

Stunt Co-ordinator The person who prepares and organises all stunts on a movie, whether they be horse falls, fights, car chases, building falls, or any action sequence which involves the possibility of an actor or stunt double getting hurt. Every move is planned and rehearsed in consultation with the director and the 1st A.D. to get the right look for the shot, but also to provide complete safety to all of the cast and crew.

Stunt Double A person who is made up and dressed to look like an actor for a stunt or action scene.

Sugar Glass A sugar based glass that was used in the past as a safe substitute for real glass.

Subjective Camera A shot or style of film that uses a specific character's point of view.

Substantial A large snack that is passed around to the crew such as a sandwich an hour or two before lunch is served.

Superimpose To blend an image right over top of another one. This may apply to titles, credits or live action photography. Godzilla was often superimposed onto a Japanese city background, as he waded through the buildings to the centre of town.

Supertechno A telescoping camera crane that comes in 30' and 50' versions. With a Supertechno you can fly the camera through a high rise apartment, out the window and down the side of the building by simply telescoping the Supertechno crane arm while remote controlling the multi-axis camera head (Flight Head). The Supertechno Crane can be used for commercials, music videos, feature films, television production, sports coverage and music concerts.

Suspense 1) To build tension in a movie by letting the audience know something is about to happen. This is done with clues in the plot, ominous music or visual clues. 2) A genre of movie that uses suspense as its main theme. Also called a *whodunit,* because the audience is trying to figure out who committed the crime.

Survey TO SET See *scout*.

Sweeps Television term. *Sweeps* refers to a ratings "sweep" of the country that occurs 4 times a year, when networks set their advertising rates based on the number of people who watch their shows. A sweeps week occurs every February, May, July and November.

Sweetening The process whereby the audio track for a film is cleaned up and prepared for a final release.

Swing Gang Construction or art department crew that assembles and takes down sets.

Swish Pan An effect in which the camera is swung very rapidly in a panning motion, producing a blurred image. Also called a *zoom pan, zip pan, flick pan, flash pan* or *whip pan*.

Switcher Person or device that takes two or more incoming video signals (usually from different cameras at, say, a hockey game) and switches between them for a broadcast of one signal.

S/W/F/H Start/Work/Finish/Hold. You will often see one or more of these letter codes near an actor's name on the call sheet or production schedule to let the crew know what their status is for any given day.

Sync Synchronise. To line up various elements such as sound effects or voice tracks so they run at the same time as a moving image.

Sync Sound Sound that is recorded simultaneously with a moving photographic image. A clapper is used to help synchronise the two in the editing process.

Syndication When a recurring show is shown as re-runs on television, it is known as *syndication*.

Synopsis A brief rundown of a script or story that may be summarised in two or three sentences.

A **Re-recording Sound Mixer** adjusts the dialogue, music and effects for the final soundtrack.
Photo Courtesy of DBC Sound, Inc. © 2010. Used with permission.

T-Bone A rigid T-shape base, usually nailed to a studio floor for low positioning of lights.

T-Stop The true f/stop number when a lens is free from reflection and absorption loss. (T means transmission and stop means to decrease the amount of light admitted to the film). A T-stop represents the f/number of a lens with 100 percent transmission of the light rays.

Table Read When the actors and director sit down at a table and read through a script prior to filming.

Taco Cart A rolling cart used by grips that has flags and other diffusion tools dangling from each side.

Tail Slate Using the clapboard or slate to "mark" the shot after a take. Usually the clapper is held upside down so an editor knows for sure it is a *tail slate*.

Take One segment of shooting during production. If the take is good, the director will often say "print," which means send the film to be processed and transferred to video to be watched the next day. These are called dailies or rushes. A bad, or "blown" take is often designated as NG, or "no good."

Talent A term used to designate the actors, musicians or stunt people in a film production.

Tapeless workflow A project that exclusively uses the digital realm for the capturing, transferring, editing and distribution of a film or video. No "tape" is ever used. See also *workflow*.

Teamster A member of the Teamster's Union. Teamsters, or "the Brothers" are responsible for driving the production vehicles on a film, including the honeywagons, starwagon, cable truck, cast vehicles, picture cars and pretty much anything else that moves.

Tearjerker A sad or heart-wrenching movie that is almost guaranteed to make you cry. See also *chick flick*

Teaser 1) The first part of a tv movie or series episode that is intended to make the viewer want to watch the show. 2) A long, thin piece of wood with a sheet of black Duvetyne cloth attached to it for shading light sources.

Technocrane A telescopic camera crane that can extend, retract or boom very smoothly for intricate, sweeping crane shots. See also *Supertechno*.

Tech Pack The package of drawings of all the floor plans for the sets and final locations on a show.

Tech Survey Once all of the locations have been selected and locked in for a production, a survey of all of the locations is attended by all of the department heads to assess each individual location's requirements and restrictions.

Teleprompter A monitor or computer screen that "prompts" a television host with their lines by printing them out on a screen that they can see but the audience can't.

Temporal Compression A technique used by filmmakers that purposely leaves out chunks of "time" in the telling of a story. A great example of this is in *2001: A Space Odyssey*, where Kubrick compresses thousands of years with the shot of an ape throwing a bone into the air cut with a shot of a spaceship.

Third Assistant Director (3rd A.D.) The person responsible for signing in and out the actors and performers on a set, making sure they get into hair, make-up and wardrobe in time for their scenes, escorting them to set, preparing the production report and assisting the 1st and 2nd A.D.'s when needed.

3-D Three-dimensional. What started in the 1950's with those funny little glasses with the green and red lenses has been enjoying a bit of renaissance lately. Keep your eyes open for more 3-D films to be released in the future.

3-D Storyboarding See pre-viz.

Three-point lighting A standard way to light a set or subject is by using a *key light* (directly on the subject), a *fill light* (from the side) and a *back light* (to create a rim of light around the subject and separate them from the background.)

Tight A shot that frames a subject very closely. (e.g., "Let's get a *tight* shot of her hand.")

Tilt A vertical camera movement, either up or down.

Time Code A code of numbers that is used to synchronise sound and picture for a film, and to keep track of the time and place of various segments during the editing process.

Time Lapse Shooting at a much slower rate than the normal time speed of 24 frames per second. This technique is often used in nature programs to show a flower growing out of the ground.

Touch Paper Paper that has been treated with potassium nitrate by the special effects crew. When touched with a cigarette or hot wire, the paper will ignite and burn along the line of solution applied to the paper. This effect has sometimes been used for main titles.

Tow Shot When filming one or more actors while driving a car, the car is often towed on a trailer to enable the actors to concentrate on acting rather than driving,and to light and shoot the scene more easily.

Tracking Shot A moving camera shot, usually achieved with a camera mounted on a dolly which is in turn mounted on a track.

Trades The newspapers and magazines that report on the film and entertainment industries, such as *Daily Variety, The Hollywood Reporter* and others.

Trailer An advertisement for a film that is shown before the screening of another film. A trailer is usually a short clip of the most stunning shots of a film edited together with sound, music and narration that says how great the film is.

Trainee Assistant Director (TAD) The trainee, or TAD, assists the other assistant directors in carrying out sometimes mundane but important tasks like getting the stars their breakfasts, issuing walkie-talkies and batteries to crew members, watching the lunch line-up, cueing extras, writing down wrap times for various crew members, handing out call sheets and other duties.

Trainee Assistant Locations (TAL) Someone who is training to be an Assistant Location Manager.

Translight A large, transparent photograph that is used as a background on soundstages. For instance, translights are used to simulate an exterior such as a skyline without having to shoot near the actual skyline.

Transport Captain The person that supervises all vehicle requirements while on set.

Transport Co-ordinator The person responsible for organising and scheduling all vehicles and drivers for a motion picture.

Trapeze A device used by grips to hang lights in mid air with ropes and pulleys.

Treatment A script form that is somewhere between a rough outline and a completed script.

Triple Threat A performer who can sing, dance and act.

Trombone A bracket that hangs on a wall to hold a small lamp.

Truck Mo The person assigned to stay in the grip, prop, lighting, camera, special effects or other film truck. Thisa person is in charge of all of the organisation of gear and inventory of the truck. Their key, or head of department will often call them on the radio to request specific pieces of gear to be ready for an upcoming shot.

Tulip Crane A small see-saw type camera crane with weights on one end and a camera and operator(s) on the other. Used for smooth sweeping and rising shots.

Tungsten A type of light filament used in lighting scenes, characterised by its orange colour tone.

Turnaround Amount of time, regulated by unions, that a production must give its crew between shooting days without going into costly penalties. (Usually 8-10 hours between days and at least 52 hours for weekends.)

A lonely **PA** guards a parking lot, waiting for the film trucks to arrive. © 2010

Turn Over See *rolling*. This term originated in Britian.

Turret A revolving disk system mounted on a camera that may be turned to use different lenses.

Turtle Base A small, three-legged base that forms the bottom of a C-stand.

Turtle Stand A stand used by the grip department that has a removable top portion to enable them to have a low stand for a light. Also called a *turtle base*.

Two-hander A shot or scene that involves a conversation between two actors.

Two-shot Camera shot that has two actors in the frame.

Tweenie A 650 watt fresnel light, the in-between (thus tweenie) of a Baby and an Inky.

Tyler Mount A gyroscopic camera mount used to film from helicopters.

Wind Machine on Location
Photo by: Joseph MacKinnon © 2010. Used with permission.

Ubangi Politically incorrect term for a mount that extends the camera away from its center on the dolly. Allegedly named for the Ubangi people of Africa who extend their lower lip by artificial means.

U.B.C.P. Union of British Columbia Performers.

Unit Manager (U.M.) Person responsible for the requirements of the crew and production when a film is complex enough to require an extensive second shooting crew or when a P.M. needs an assistant for extra duties.

Umbrella Light A lighting device that employs a white mylar umbrella with a tungsten-halogen light attached to its handle and pointing into the centre of the umbrella. This type of soft light is often used as a window light source because of its "wrap around" quality.

Upstage 1) That portion of a set furthest away from the camera. 2) To try to get all of the attention away from another actor.

V

Variac Trade name of a variable transformer (dimmer control) used by the lighting and special effects departments.

Vertigo Shot A camera shot that zooms forward with the lens while tracking or dollying backward. This shot, which conveys a feeling of dizziness, was created for Alfred Hitchcock's masterpiece *Vertigo* by second-unit cameraman Irmin Roberts. It is one of the most widely imitated shots in film history.

Video Assist A video monitor that connects to the 35mm film camera allowing the director to watch a take as it is being filmed.

Video Sync The synchronisation of an image from a tv or computer screen to conform with the 24 fps used by the cameras. If you don't have video sync, you get annoying scan lines moving up or down the screen on the film or video image.

Video Village The area set up on a film shoot that has monitors set up for the director, producers and other crew to watch shots as they are being filmed or just after.

Viewfinder The part of a camera that you look through to see the image.

Vignette 1) A shot that is blurry or fuzzy around the edges and clear and focused in the middle. 2) A short segment of a story.

Visual Effects Computer graphics and animation that are added in after filming is completed. Also called *VFX*.

Vodcasting Video podcasting. A digital form of a movie or tv show that is made available for download and viewing from home computers, cell phones, PDAs and other devices

Voice Over (V.O.) An audible narration layered into the soundtrack.

A helicopter with a **SpaceCam** gyroscopic camera mount lifts off in preparation for a smooth **aerial shot**.
Photo courtesy of SpaceCam Systems Inc. © 2010. Used with Permission.

W

Walk and Talk Common shot that involves people walking and talking. This is a great way to kill off a big dialogue scene with some movement, used quite often on tv movies.

Walla The name given to a track of ambient sound that is layered onto a film, such as the sound of people in a restaurant or sports event to create a "wall" of sound.

Wall Sled A device used by grips to hang lights and other equipment from a wall.

Wardrobe Department The group of people on a crew that are in charge of dressing actors, background performers and anyone else that wears clothing. Also called the *costume department*.

Warm Prop Slang term for an *extra,* or *background performer.*

Weather Cover See *Cover Set.*

Western Dolly Similar in design to a doorway dolly, the western is larger and capable of carrying a heavier load. It can be used as a camera dolly, equipment mover or as a tow platform behind a camera car.

Wedges Small triangular blocks of wood used by grips to elevate or level dolly tracks, apple boxes or other pieces of film gear.

Wescam A camera stabilising device that is used for extremely smooth aerial shots.

Wetdown The dousing of any part of a set (usually streets at night) to create a glossy, reflective look on film.

W.G.A. Writer's Guild of America.

W.G.C. Writer's Guild of Canada.

Wide Screen An aspect ratio that has a larger width than height, such as 16 by 9. See also *letterbox*.

Wide Shot One that is the opposite of a close up, one that covers a lot of area in the frame.

Wild Line (or Wild Track) Sound or dialogue recorded on a set without any cameras rolling, usually to record ambient environment sounds, or to get a better dialogue line.

Wild Wall, Wild Ceilings Walls and ceilings that can be moved on a set at any given moment.

Windjammer Fuzzy tube shaped item placed over a microphone at the end of a boom to decrease wind noise.

Window Shot The last shot of the day. One of the happiest things you can hear after a 15 hour day. ("O.K. everybody, this is the *window shot*, so let's concentrate.") Some people say the term arose out of "when do we go?" but the actual meaning goes back to London in the early, early days of filmmaking when everyone on the crew was paid in cash daily. After the last shot was completed they went to the window to get their payment. Also called a *martini shot* in the U.S.

Winnies Winnebagos. On smaller shoots and some commercials, winnebagos or motor homes are used instead of more costly trailers. The Winnie can be the honeywagon, A.D. box, conference room, wardrobe trailer, and production office all in one. Also called a *moho*.

Wipe 1) An actor or vehicle that crosses the camera frame horizontally. 2) An edit that "wipes" one shot into the next from right to left or vice-versa.

Wire A small microphone and transmitter that is attached to an actor, whose dialogue is then mixed by the sound mixer along with sound recorded by a boom operator. Also called a *lav*, or *lavalier microphone*, *radio microphone* or *body mic*.

Wire Work Scenes that involve actors or stunt performers to "fly" around a set or location with the help of wires attached to a body harness. Film such as *Crouching Tiger, Hidden Dragon* and the *Matrix* films feature elaborate *wire work* within their fight scenes.

Wish List A list created by a director, producer or writer of their top picks of people to work on their film. For a director, it might mean a list of their favourite actors for various roles, or for a writer it might be a list of the top directors they would like to work with, and so on.

Workflow The use of different formats or media during the shooting, editing and distribution phases of a movie or tv show. For example, a movie may be shot on film, transferred to a digital format for editing and visual effects, and then transferred back to film to be shown in theatres. This is called the *workflow*.

Work Print A copy of the footage from a movie or tv show that can be used to try out editing ideas.

Work-through Lunch An agreement by which the crew works past the regularly scheduled lunch break because of outdoor light or to finish a scene or shot that needs a little bit more time.

Work Trucks The trucks that are worked out of the most—the grip truck, the camera truck, the lighting truck, the FX truck and the props truck. These vehicles are usually parked as close to the set as possible.

Working Title A title given to a project as it is being worked on that may or may not become the actual title of a film.

Wrap The happiest word on a movie set. Done for the day. Finished. Go home and get your three or four hours of sleep.

Wrap Party The party that is generally held after the completion of a film or tv series.

Wrangler Person who "wrangles" extras, animals or livestock during the shooting of a film, or person who rounds them up before a shoot.

Xenon Lamp  A special type of light that uses a xenon filament.

X-Rated A pornographic or ultra violent film, now referred to as NC-17 by the American standards board.

X-sheet Animation filming sheet with written exposure specs.

Sound Mixing Room or **Dub Stage**
Photo courtesy of DBC Sound. © 2010. Used with permission.

Yagi Fold up antenna device used by the sound department when wireless microphones are employed.

Y-Cable Cable that splits one signal into two, or vice-versa.

Yellow Light When a producer has a portion of the money raised to fund a project, allowing them to get to the next step of financing. See also *green light* and *step deal*.

A boom operator records an actor's dialogue on location. Photo courtesy of Eric Batut. © 2010. Used with permission.

Z

Zeppelin Windscreen A blimp-shaped cover that fits over a microphone boom to prevent wind sounds from interfering with the recording.

Zinger Any directional light source used to highlight a scene predominantly lit with soft light.

Zip A 2000 watt narrow softlight, useful in low ceiling situations.

Zoetrope A machine invented in the 1800's that was one of the first motion picture projection devices. Incidentally, Francis Coppola's film company is called *American Zoetrope*.

Zoom 1) A lens movement in or out of a scene. 2) The lens used to perform this movement.

"For those in the industry or those who want to be in the know, Vancouver's all-around film guy Tim Moshansky has just published the **A to Z Guide to Film Terms**. Chock full of technical jargon and slang expressions, the guide has become a Canadian best-seller and required reading in some university and college film programs."

—Maclean's Magazine

"The **A to Z Guide to Film Terms** is a great, pocket sized resource book for anyone in the film biz. I have used it in my film orientation classes for the past 10 years and recommend it to all newcomers to the industry. It's an invaluable tool."

—Jane Still, Set Etiquette and Costuming Instructor at Capilano College Film Program.

"The **A to Z Guide to Film Terms** has been a best-seller at Biz Books from the day it arrived. This pocket-sized book appeals to a whole cross-section of our customers – from the new actor or crew member anticipating their first day on set to the film buff who just wants to be 'in the know'. It is such a valued resource that many schools, teachers, and professional training facilities make this required reading for their students.

Affordable and informative – it's one of our top recommendations."

—Catherine Lough-Haggquist, Film and Television Actor and Owner of Biz Books in Vancouver, BC

"As a producer/director, and filmmaking instructor, I have used the booklet **A to Z Guide to Film Terms** many times in a classroom situation and have found it to be an excellent resource to the language of film."

—Roy Hayter, Director, Producer and Instructor at the Vancouver Film School

"This handy guide may be required reading at some university and college film programs, but it's also great for any film buff who has watched the credits roll at the end of a movie and wondered just what the heck a gaffer is. (A gaffer is the person in charge of all electrical and light requirements on a set.)"

—Tribute Magazine

"Although there are various guides floating around the place, the aptly named **A to Z Guide to Film Terms** stands tall above these, both for its comprehensiveness and for the fact it is more than just a dictionary - it has numerous real life examples, written from a true insider's perspective. And it's pocket-friendly size means that new and not-so-new filmmakers can keep it handy for a sneak peak on set when the need arises.

—Filmmaking.net

This little encyclopedia is great for beginning filmmakers in school, and for experienced auteurs who forget the terms used by their colleagues. It fits easily into trouser or tote pocket so there is no struggle retrieving it when needed. Even the layout is good so there is no problem finding the terms you need, and the type is easy on the eye. This modest book fills a big need, and it's a charmer.

—Eleanore Speert, The Drama Book Shop, Inc., New York City

Walkie-talkie talk

Where would filmmaking be without walkie-talkies (radios)? These are the lifelines of communication on a working film shoot. Sometimes people clip them onto their belts, some wear headsets (especially the A.D.'s) and some have those fancy harness units that hold them at your chest for easy reach.

There is a certain protocol people follow when talking on the radios. You can always tell when someone gets on and hasn't done it before. We've all heard the faux pas on the walkies. Don't be one of the guys (or girls) everyone glares at when someone calls for you and you've got your volume cranked up right near the set during a take.

Here's a quick guide to the walkie-talk you'll need to know. By the way, if you need a new battery, ask one of the A.D.'s. Copy that?

10-4 Affirmative. Yes, I got your message and I am confirming it. Also used: "*Roger*" and "copy that."

10-20 Current location. "What's your 20," means, "Where are you?"

10-100 Going to the bathroom. Nature calls. Sometimes shortened to "*Ten-one*."

Copy I got your message and I understand. "*Copy that*" is often used as well.

Go for me A common response to give when someone calls for you or your department on the radio. Also used: "Go for (*insert first name*)" or, "Go for (*name of department*)."

Go to "2" Adjust your walkie channel control to channel 2. Channel 1 is reserved as an open channel for the crew to announce "cuts" and "rolls" etc. Channel 2 is used for longer conversations and idle chatter that the rest of the crew does not need to hear. It is acceptable to ask someone to "go to 2," on channel 1, but not during a take. Typical talk on channel 1 would be something like this: "Hi, Joe Special Effects?" "Go for Joe." "Hi Joe, can you go to 2?" "*Going to 2*."

Walkie Check This can be announced on Channel 1 to make sure your radio is working.

A to Z Guide to Film Terms

From the Author

I have worked in the film industry for nearly 25 years. Starting as a Locations P.A. in the late 1980's, I have since worked in various roles over the years including Extras Wrangler, Boom Operator, Grip and Location Scout. I have had the opportunity to work with many talented people over the years on dozens of projects, and I hope to pass some of this knowledge to you.

About the Book

The A to Z Guide started out as a 56-page, staple-bound book with a print run of 250 copies. Since then, the book has travelled the world, and is used as a textbook for film students across Canada and the U.S. To date more than 25,000 copies have been sold, and it's still a hit on the set.

To order more copies visit:
www.filmterms.com

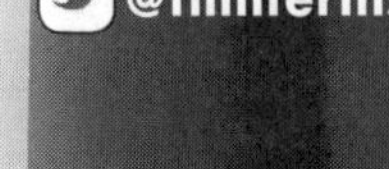

e-book formats available:
www.Amazon.com &
www.Smashwords.com